asian

100 EASY RECIPES
asian

bay books

contents

small food

thai potato cakes

750 g (1 lb 10 oz) boiling potatoes, peeled
1–2 small red chillies, finely chopped
8 cm (3¼ inch) piece lemongrass,
   white part only, finely chopped
3 very large handfuls coriander (cilantro)
   leaves, chopped
8 spring onions (scallions), chopped
2 eggs, lightly beaten
3 tablespoons plain (all-purpose) flour
oil, for shallow-frying
sweet chilli sauce, for serving

serves 4

method   Grate the potatoes, then squeeze dry in a tea towel (dish towel) to remove as much moisture as possible. Mix with the chilli, lemongrass, coriander, spring onion, egg and flour.

Heat 1.5 cm (5/8 inch) of oil in a frying pan. Use 2 heaped tablespoons of mixture to make each cake and cook three or four cakes at a time, for 3–4 minutes over medium heat. Turn and cook for another 3 minutes, or until crisp and cooked through. Drain on paper towels and keep warm while cooking the remaining mixture. Serve hot with sweet chilli sauce.

satay chicken

500 g (1 lb 2 oz) boneless, skinless
chicken thighs
1 onion, roughly chopped
2 lemongrass stems, white part only,
thinly sliced
4 garlic cloves
2 red chillies, chopped
2 teaspoons ground coriander
1 teaspoon ground cumin
1 tablespoon soy sauce
3 tablespoons oil, or as needed
1 tablespoon soft brown sugar
cucumber slices and chopped roasted
peanuts, to garnish

peanut sauce

125 g (5 oz/½ cup) crunchy peanut butter
250 ml (9 fl oz/1 cup) coconut milk
1–2 tablespoons sweet chilli sauce
1 tablespoon soy sauce
2 teaspoons lemon juice

serves 4

method Soak 20 wooden skewers in cold water for 30 minutes to prevent scorching. Cut the chicken into 20 thick flat strips and thread onto the skewers.

Mix the onion, lemongrass, garlic, chilli, coriander, cumin, ½ teaspoon of salt and soy sauce in a food processor until smooth, adding a little oil if necessary. Spread the mixture over the chicken, cover and refrigerate for 30 minutes.

To make the peanut sauce, stir all the ingredients and 125 ml (4 fl oz/½ cup) water over low heat, until the mixture boils. Remove from the heat. The sauce will thicken on standing.

Brush a very hot chargrill pan or barbecue flat plate with the remaining oil. Cook the skewers in batches for 2–3 minutes on each side, sprinkling with a little oil and brown sugar. Serve with the peanut sauce, cucumber slices and chopped peanuts, if desired.

spring rolls

2 tablespoons oil
2 garlic cloves, chopped
2.5 cm (1 inch) piece fresh ginger, grated
100 g (4 oz) lean minced (ground) pork
100 g (4 oz) minced (ground) chicken
60 g (2 oz) raw minced (ground) prawns
    (shrimp)
2 celery stalks, finely sliced
1 small carrot, finely chopped
90 g (3 oz/½ cup) chopped water chestnuts
4 spring onions (scallions), chopped
75 g (3 oz/1 cup) finely shredded cabbage
125 ml (4 fl oz/½ cup) chicken stock
4 tablespoons cornflour (cornstarch)
2 tablespoons oyster sauce
1 tablespoon soy sauce
2 teaspoons sesame oil
36 small square spring roll wrappers
oil, for deep-frying
sweet chilli sauce, for serving

makes 18

method   Heat 1 tablespoon oil in a wok or frying pan and cook the garlic and ginger for 30 seconds. Add the minced pork, chicken and prawn and cook for 3 minutes, or until they are brown. Transfer to a bowl.

Wipe the pan, then heat the remaining tablespoon of oil. Add the celery, carrot, water chestnuts, spring onion and cabbage and stir over medium heat for 2 minutes. Combine the stock, 1 tablespoon of the cornflour, oyster and soy sauces and salt and pepper, add to the vegetables and stir until thickened. Stir the sesame oil and vegetables into the meat mixture and allow to cool. Mix the remaining cornflour with 4 tablespoons water until smooth.

Put 1 spring roll wrapper on a work surface with one corner towards you. Brush the edges with a little cornflour paste and cover with another wrapper. Brush the edges of the second wrapper and spread about 1½ tablespoons of the filling across the bottom corner of the wrapper. Fold the bottom corner up over the filling, fold in the sides and roll up firmly. Repeat with the remaining wrappers and filling. Heat the oil in a deep saucepan and fry the rolls, in batches, for 2–3 minutes, or until golden. Drain and serve with sweet chilli sauce.

won ton wrapped prawns

24 raw prawns (shrimp)
1 teaspoon cornflour (cornstarch)
24 won ton wrappers
oil, for deep-frying
125 ml (4 fl oz/½ cup) sweet chilli sauce
1 tablespoon lime juice

makes 24

method Peel and devein the prawns, leaving the tails intact.

Mix the cornflour with 1 teaspoon water in a small bowl. Work with one won ton wrapper at a time, keeping the rest covered with a damp tea towel (dish towel) to prevent drying out. Fold a wrapper in half to form a triangle. Wrap a prawn in the wrapper, leaving the tail exposed. Seal at the end by brushing with a little of the cornflour mixture, then pressing gently. Spread the wrapped prawns on a baking tray, cover with plastic wrap and refrigerate for 20 minutes.

Fill a deep heavy-based saucepan one-third full of oil and heat to 180°C (350°F), or until a cube of bread dropped into the oil browns in 15 seconds. Cook the prawns in batches for 1½ minutes each batch, or until crisp, golden and cooked through. The cooking time may vary depending on the size of the prawns. Check the time by cooking one prawn and testing it before continuing. Remove the prawns from the oil with a slotted spoon and drain on crumpled paper towels.

Stir the sweet chilli sauce and lime juice together in a small bowl. Serve with the prawns.

tofu kebabs with miso pesto

1 large red capsicum (pepper), cut into squares
12 button mushrooms, halved
6 baby onions, quartered
3 zucchini (courgettes), thickly sliced
450 g (1 lb) firm tofu, cut into small cubes
125 ml (4 fl oz/½ cup) olive oil
3 tablespoons soy sauce
2 garlic cloves, crushed
2 teaspoons grated fresh ginger

miso pesto

90 g (3 oz) unsalted roasted peanuts
3 very large handfuls coriander (cilantro) leaves
2 tablespoons shiro miso (white miso)
2 garlic cloves
100 ml (4 fl oz) olive oil

serves 4

method   Soak 12 wooden skewers in cold water for 30 minutes to prevent scorching. Thread the vegetable pieces and tofu alternately onto the skewers, then place in a large shallow non-metallic dish.

Combine the olive oil, soy sauce, garlic and ginger, then pour half the mixture over the kebabs. Cover with plastic wrap and marinate for 1 hour.

To make the miso pesto, finely chop the peanuts, coriander leaves, miso paste and garlic in a food processor. Slowly add the olive oil while the machine is still running and blend to a smooth paste.

Heat a chargrill pan or barbecue flat plate and cook the kebabs, turning and brushing often with the remaining marinade, for 4–6 minutes, or until the edges are slightly brown. Serve with the miso pesto.

sesame tempura prawns

soy dipping sauce

1 tablespoon grated fresh ginger
250 ml (9 fl oz/1 cup) Japanese soy sauce
1 tablespoon sesame seeds, toasted
1 tablespoon caster (superfine) sugar

oil, for deep-frying
125 g (5 oz/1 cup) tempura flour
2 tablespoons sesame seeds
750 g (1 lb 10 oz) raw prawns (shrimp), peeled
and deveined, tails left intact

serves 6

method Combine the soy dipping sauce ingredients in a small bowl.

Fill a deep, heavy-based saucepan one-third full of oil and heat to 180°C (350°F), until a cube of bread dropped in the oil browns in 15 seconds. Place the tempura flour and the sesame seeds in a bowl and gradually stir in 185 ml (6 fl oz/3/4 cup) iced water with chopsticks until just combined. (The batter should still be lumpy.)

Dip the prawns, 3–4 at a time, into the batter and deep-fry for 1–2 minutes, until golden brown. Drain on crumpled paper towels and serve at once with the dipping sauce.

california rolls

500 g (1 lb 2 oz/2¼ cups) short-grain white rice
3 tablespoons rice vinegar
1 tablespoon caster (superfine) sugar
5 sheets nori (dried seaweed)
1 large Lebanese (short) cucumber, cut
    lengthways into long batons
1 avocado, thinly sliced
1 tablespoon black sesame seeds, toasted
30 g (1 oz) pickled ginger slices
125 g (5 oz/½ cup) mayonnaise
3 teaspoons wasabi paste
2 teaspoons soy sauce

makes 30

method   Wash the rice under cold running water, tossing, until the water runs clear. Put the rice and 750 ml (26 fl oz/3 cups) water in a saucepan. Bring to the boil over low heat and cook for 5 minutes, or until tunnels form in the rice. Remove from the heat, cover and leave for 15 minutes.

Place the vinegar, sugar and 1 teaspoon salt in a small saucepan and stir over low heat until the sugar and salt dissolve.

Transfer the rice to a non-metallic bowl and use a wooden spoon to separate the grains. Make a slight well in the centre, slowly stir in the vinegar dressing, then cool a little.

Lay a nori sheet, shiny side down, on a bamboo mat or flat surface and spread out one-fifth of the rice, leaving a clear border at one end. Arrange one-fifth of the cucumber, avocado, sesame seeds and ginger lengthways over the rice, to within 2.5 cm (1 inch) of the border. Spread with some of the combined mayonnaise, wasabi and soy sauce and roll to cover the filling. Continue rolling tightly to join the edges, then hold in place for a few seconds. Trim the ends and cut into slices. Serve with wasabi mayonnaise.

san choy bau

1 tablespoon peanut oil
1 teaspoon sesame oil
1–2 garlic cloves, crushed
1 tablespoon grated fresh ginger
4 spring onions (scallions), chopped
500 g (1 lb 2 oz) lean minced (ground) pork
1 red capsicum (pepper), seeded and diced
220 g (8 oz) tin water chestnuts, drained and roughly chopped
1–2 tablespoons soy sauce
1 tablespoon oyster sauce
2 tablespoons dry sherry
4 iceberg lettuce leaves

serves 4

method Heat the oils in a large, non-stick frying pan or wok. Add the garlic, ginger and spring onion and stir-fry for about 2 minutes. Add the minced pork and cook over medium heat until well browned, breaking up any lumps with a fork or wooden spoon.

Stir in the capsicum, water chestnuts, soy and oyster sauces and sherry. Simmer over medium heat until the liquid reduces and thickens. Keep warm.

Trim the edges of the lettuce leaves to make cup shapes, then spoon the pork into the lettuce leaves.

vegetable tempura patties

wasabi mayonnaise

2 teaspoons wasabi paste
1 teaspoon Japanese soy sauce
125 g (5 oz/½ cup) mayonnaise
1 teaspoon sake

½ carrot, cut into thin strips
½ onion, thinly sliced
100 g (4 oz) orange sweet potato, grated
1 small zucchini (courgette), grated
1 small potato, cut into thin strips
4 spring onions (scallions), cut into matchsticks
4 sheets nori (dried seaweed), shredded
250 g (9 oz/2 cups) tempura flour, sifted
500 ml (17 fl oz/2 cups) chilled soda water
oil, for deep-frying
2 tablespoons shredded pickled ginger

serves 4

method To make the wasabi mayonnaise, stir together all the ingredients.

To make the patties, place the carrot, onion, orange sweet potato, zucchini, potato, spring onion and nori in a bowl. Toss together.

Place the tempura flour in a large bowl and make a well in the centre. Add the soda water and loosely mix together with chopsticks or a fork until just combined—the batter should still be lumpy. Add the vegetables and quickly fold through until just combined with the batter.

Fill a wok or deep heavy-based saucepan one-third full of oil and heat it to 180°C (350°F). Gently drop a heaped tablespoon of the vegetable mixture into the oil and cook until golden. Drain on paper towels and season with sea salt. Repeat with the remaining mixture to make 12 patties. Serve immediately, topped with the wasabi mayonnaise and the pickled ginger.

chicken skewers with mango salsa

4 boneless, skinless chicken thighs
1½ tablespoons soft brown sugar
1½ tablespoons lime juice
2 teaspoons green curry paste
18 makrut (kaffir lime) leaves
2 lemongrass stems

mango salsa

1 small mango, finely diced
1 teaspoon grated lime zest
2 teaspoons lime juice
1 teaspoon soft brown sugar
½ teaspoon fish sauce

serves 4

method   Cut the chicken thighs in half lengthways. Combine the brown sugar, lime juice, curry paste and two shredded makrut leaves in a bowl. Add the chicken and mix well. Cover and refrigerate for at least 4 hours.

Trim the lemongrass to measure 20 cm (8 inches), leaving the root end intact. Cut each lengthways into four pieces. Cut a slit in each of the remaining makrut leaves and then thread one onto each lemongrass skewer. Cut two slits in each piece of chicken and then thread onto the lemongrass, followed by another makrut leaf. Repeat with the remaining makrut leaves, chicken and lemongrass. Pan-fry or barbecue until cooked through.

Gently stir together all the ingredients for the mango salsa and serve with the chicken skewers.

salt-and-pepper squid

1 kg (2 lb 4 oz) squid tubes, halved lengthways
250 ml (9 fl oz/1 cup) lemon juice
125 g (5 oz/1 cup) cornflour (cornstarch)
1 tablespoon ground white pepper
2 teaspoons caster (superfine) sugar
4 egg whites, lightly beaten
oil, for deep-frying
lemon wedges, to serve

serves 6

method   Open out the squid tubes, wash and pat dry. Score a shallow diamond pattern on the inside, then cut into 5 x 3 cm (2 x 1¼ inch) pieces. Place in a flat non-metallic dish and pour over the lemon juice. Cover and refrigerate for 15 minutes. Drain well and pat dry.

Combine the cornflour, 1½ tablespoons of salt, white pepper and sugar in a bowl. Dip the squid in the egg white and lightly coat with the cornflour mixture, shaking off any excess.

Fill a deep heavy-based saucepan one-third full of oil and heat to 180°C (350°F), until a cube of bread dropped into the oil turns golden brown in 15 seconds. Deep-fry the squid, in batches, for 1 minute each batch, or until the squid turns white and curls up. Drain on crumpled paper towels. Serve with the lemon wedges.

thai meatballs

350 g (12 oz) minced (ground) beef
3 French shallots (eschalots), finely chopped
3 garlic cloves, chopped
2.5 cm (1 inch) piece fresh ginger, grated
1 tablespoon green or pink peppercorns,
crushed
2 teaspoons light soy sauce
2 teaspoons fish sauce
2 teaspoons soft brown sugar
1 very large handful coriander (cilantro) leaves
lime wedges
1 Lebanese (short) cucumber, chopped
3 sliced red or green chillies

serves 4

method   Chop the minced beef with a cleaver or a large knife until very fine. Mix together the beef, shallots, garlic, ginger, peppercorns, light soy sauce, fish sauce and brown sugar.

Form 2 teaspoons of the mixture at a time into balls. Thread the balls onto eight wooden skewers, using three balls for each skewer.

Cook the skewers on a hot oiled chargrill pan or barbecue flat plate for 8 minutes, turning frequently, until cooked through. Sprinkle with coriander. Serve with the lime wedges, cucumber and chillies.

hint   *Soak the wooden skewers in cold water for at least 30 minutes before use to prevent scorching.*

miso yakitori chicken

1 kg (2 lb 4 oz) chicken thighs, skin on
3 tablespoons yellow or red miso paste
2 tablespoons sugar
3 tablespoons sake
2 tablespoons mirin
1 Lebanese (short) cucumber
2 spring onions (scallions), cut into
   short lengths

serves 4

method Remove the bones from the chicken. Meanwhile, soak 12 wooden skewers in cold water for 30 minutes to prevent scorching. Place the miso, sugar, sake and mirin in a small saucepan over medium heat and cook, stirring well, for 2 minutes, or until the sauce is smooth.

Cut the chicken into bite-sized cubes. Seed the cucumber and cut into small batons. Thread the chicken, cucumber and spring onion alternately onto the skewers, using three pieces of each per skewer.

Cook on a chargrill pan or barbecue grill plate over high heat, turning occasionally, for 10 minutes, or until the chicken is almost cooked through. Brush with the miso sauce and continue cooking, then turn and brush the other side. Repeat once or twice until the chicken and vegetables are cooked through. Serve immediately.

thai fish cakes

500 g (1 lb 2 oz) red fish fillets, chopped
1 lemongrass stem, white part only, chopped
2 tablespoons fish sauce
5 spring onions (scallions), chopped
3 tablespoons chopped coriander (cilantro)
1 garlic clove, crushed
150 ml (5 fl oz) tin coconut milk
1 tablespoon sweet chilli sauce
1 egg
5 snake (yard long) beans, thinly sliced
oil, for shallow-frying

sauce

90 g (3 oz) sugar
2 tablespoons sweet chilli sauce
½ small Lebanese (short) cucumber, diced

serves 6

method   Place the fish, lemongrass, fish sauce, spring onion, coriander, garlic, coconut milk, sweet chilli sauce and egg in a food processor and mix until smooth. Transfer to a bowl and fold in the snake beans. With wet hands, shape into twelve 8 cm (3¼ inch) cakes. Cover on a plate and refrigerate until ready to use.

For the sauce, stir the sugar and 4 tablespoons water in a small saucepan over low heat for 2 minutes, or until all the sugar has dissolved. Increase the heat and simmer for 5 minutes, until slightly thickened. Remove from the heat and stir in the sweet chilli sauce. Cool and stir in the diced cucumber.

Heat the oil in a large, deep, heavy-based frying pan and cook the fish cakes in batches over medium heat for 1–2 minutes on each side, or until cooked through. Serve with the sauce.

noodles
and rice

chicken noodle soup

3 dried Chinese mushrooms
185 g (7 oz) dried thin egg noodles
1 tablespoon oil
4 spring onions (scallions), cut into fine shreds
1 tablespoon soy sauce
2 tablespoons rice wine, mirin or sherry
1.25 litres (44 fl oz/5 cups) chicken stock
½ small barbecued chicken, shredded
60 g (2 oz) sliced ham, cut into strips
90 g (3 oz/1 cup) bean sprouts
coriander (cilantro) leaves and thinly sliced
    red chilli, to garnish

serves 4

method   Soak the mushrooms in boiling water for 10 minutes to soften them. Squeeze dry, then remove the tough stems from the mushrooms and slice the caps thinly.

Cook the noodles in a large pan of boiling water for 3 minutes, or according to the packet directions. Drain and cut the noodles into shorter lengths with scissors.

Heat the oil in a large heavy-based saucepan. Add the mushrooms and shredded spring onion. Cook for 1 minute, then add the soy sauce, rice wine and chicken stock. Bring slowly to the boil and then cook for 1 minute. Reduce the heat then add the noodles, shredded chicken, ham and bean sprouts. Heat through for 2 minutes without allowing to boil.

Use tongs to divide the noodles among four bowls, ladle in the remaining mixture, and garnish with coriander leaves and sliced chilli.

note   *Rice wine and mirin are available at Asian food stores.*

soba noodle soup

250 g (9 oz) soba noodles
2 dried shiitake mushrooms
2 litres (8 cups) vegetable stock
120 g (4 oz) snow peas (mangetouts),
thinly sliced
2 small carrots, cut into thin strips
6 spring onions (scallions), cut into short
lengths and thinly sliced lengthways
2 garlic cloves, finely chopped
2.5 cm (1 inch) piece fresh ginger,
finely shredded
4 tablespoons soy sauce
3 tablespoons mirin or sake
90 g (3 oz/1 cup) bean sprouts

serves 4

method Cook the noodles according to the packet instructions and drain.

Soak the mushrooms in 125 ml (4 fl oz/$\frac{1}{2}$ cup) boiling water until soft. Drain, reserving the liquid. Remove the stalks and slice the mushroom caps.

Combine the vegetable stock, mushrooms, mushroom liquid, snow peas, carrot, spring onion, garlic and ginger in a large saucepan. Bring slowly to the boil, then reduce the heat to low and simmer for 5 minutes, or until the vegetables are tender. Add the soy sauce, mirin and bean sprouts. Cook for a further 3 minutes.

Divide the noodles among four large serving bowls. Ladle the hot liquid and vegetables over the top and serve immediately.

thai-style chicken and corn soup

2 litres (8 cups) chicken stock
425 g (15 oz) tin corn kernels, undrained
8 spring onions (scallions), sliced
1 tablespoon finely chopped fresh ginger
4 small boneless, skinless chicken breasts, finely sliced
1 tablespoon sweet chilli sauce
1 tablespoon fish sauce
120 g (4 oz) rice vermicelli noodles
1 very large handful coriander (cilantro) leaves, chopped
2 teaspoons grated lime zest
2 tablespoons lime juice

serves 4

method Bring the chicken stock to the boil in a large saucepan over high heat. Add the corn kernels and liquid, spring onion and ginger, then reduce the heat and simmer for 1 minute.

Add the chicken, sweet chilli sauce and fish sauce and simmer for 3 minutes, or until the chicken is cooked through.

Meanwhile, put the noodles in a heatproof bowl and pour in enough boiling water to cover. Leave for 4 minutes, or until softened. Drain the noodles and cut them into shorter lengths.

Add the noodles, coriander, lime zest and lime juice to the soup and serve immediately.

vietnamese salad

200 g (7 oz) dried rice vermicelli
140 g (5 oz/1 cup) crushed peanuts
1 large handful Vietnamese mint leaves, torn
1 very large handful coriander (cilantro) leaves
½ red onion, cut into thin wedges
1 green mango, cut into matchsticks
1 Lebanese (short) cucumber, halved
lengthways and thinly sliced

lemongrass dressing

125 ml (4 fl oz/½ cup) lime juice
1 tablespoon shaved palm sugar (jaggery)
3 tablespoons seasoned rice vinegar
2 lemongrass stems, finely chopped
2 red chillies, seeded and finely chopped
3 makrut (kaffir lime) leaves, shredded

serves 4–6

method Place the rice vermicelli in a bowl and cover with boiling water. Leave for 10 minutes, or until soft, then drain, rinse under cold water and cut into short lengths.

Place the vermicelli, three-quarters of the peanuts, the mint, coriander, onion, mango and cucumber in a large bowl and toss together.

To make the dressing, place all the ingredients in a jar with a lid and shake together.

Toss the salad and dressing and refrigerate for 30 minutes. Sprinkle with the remaining nuts to serve.

hokkien noodle salad

900 g (2 lb) hokkien (egg) noodles
6 spring onions (scallions), sliced diagonally
1 large red capsicum (pepper), thinly sliced
200 g (7 oz/2 cups) snow peas (mangetouts),
    sliced
1 carrot, thinly sliced diagonally
3 very large handfuls mint, chopped
3 very large handfuls coriander (cilantro),
    chopped
100 g (4 oz/$\frac{2}{3}$ cup) roasted cashew nuts

sesame dressing

2 teaspoons sesame oil
1 tablespoon peanut oil
2 tablespoons lime juice
2 tablespoons kecap manis (see Note)
3 tablespoons sweet chilli sauce

serves 8

method   Gently separate the noodles and place in a large bowl, cover with boiling water and leave for 2 minutes. Rinse and drain.

Put the noodles in a large bowl. Add the spring onion, capsicum, snow peas, carrot, mint and coriander. Toss together well.

To make the dressing, whisk together the oils, lime juice, kecap manis and sweet chilli sauce. Pour the dressing over the salad and toss again. Sprinkle the cashew nuts over the top and serve immediately.

note   *Kecap manis is a thick, sweet soy sauce available from Asian grocery stores. If you cannot find it, use regular soy sauce with a little soft brown sugar added, as a substitute.*

vietnamese chicken salad

3 boneless, skinless chicken breasts
1 red chilli, seeded and finely chopped
3 tablespoons lime juice
2 tablespoons soft brown sugar
3 tablespoons fish sauce
½ Chinese cabbage, shredded
2 carrots, grated
3 very large handfuls mint, shredded

serves 4

method Put the chicken in a saucepan, cover with water and bring to the boil, then reduce the heat and simmer for 10 minutes, or until cooked through.

While the chicken is cooking, mix together the red chilli, lime juice, sugar and fish sauce. Remove the chicken from the water. Cool slightly, then shred into small pieces.

Combine the chicken, cabbage, carrot, mint and dressing. Toss well and serve immediately.

storage *Any leftovers can be used the next day in a stir-fry.*

sichuan chicken and noodle salad

5 cm (2 inch) piece fresh ginger, thinly sliced
5 spring onions (scallions)
2 chicken breasts, with bone and skin
1 teaspoon sichuan peppercorns (or whole
   black peppercorns)
250 g (9 oz) shanghai wheat noodles
1 teaspoon sesame oil
1 tablespoon light soy sauce
2 Lebanese (short) cucumbers, cut in half
   lengthways and thinly sliced
1½ tablespoons lime juice
1 very large handful coriander (cilantro) leaves
lime wedges, to serve

serves 4

method Bring a large saucepan of water to the boil. Add the ginger, 2 spring onions, thinly sliced, and 2 teaspoons salt and simmer for 10 minutes. Add the chicken and simmer gently for 15–20 minutes. Remove the chicken from the pan. When it is cool enough to handle, remove the skin and bones, then finely shred the flesh—there should be about 300 g (11 oz) of shredded chicken. Place in a bowl and cover with plastic wrap. Refrigerate until ready to use.

Dry-roast the peppercorns and 1 teaspoon salt in a small non-stick frying pan over medium–high heat for 5 minutes, stirring constantly, until the salt begins to darken. Remove from the heat and cool. When cool, grind the salt and pepper mixture in a spice grinder or mortar and pestle, until very fine.

Cook the noodles in a saucepan of boiling water for 4–5 minutes, or until tender. Drain well and rinse under cold water. Place the noodles in a large bowl and toss with the sesame oil and soy sauce.

Sprinkle the salt and pepper mixture over the chicken and toss well, covering as much of the chicken as possible with the spice mixture. Thinly slice the remaining spring onions, then add them to the chicken mixture with the cucumber and toss well. Add the chicken mixture and lime juice to the noodles and toss together. Top with the coriander and serve with lime wedges.

thai prawn and noodle salad

dressing

2 tablespoons grated fresh ginger
2 tablespoons soy sauce
2 tablespoons sesame oil
4 tablespoons red wine vinegar
1 tablespoon sweet chilli sauce
2 garlic cloves, crushed
4 tablespoons kecap manis
(see Note, page 28)

500 g (1 lb 2 oz) cooked large prawns (shrimp)
250 g (9 oz) dried instant egg noodles
5 spring onions (scallions), sliced diagonally
2 tablespoons chopped coriander (cilantro)
1 red capsicum (pepper), diced
100 g (4 oz/1 cup) snow peas
(mangetouts), sliced
lime wedges, to serve

serves 4

method For the dressing, whisk together the ginger, soy sauce, sesame oil, vinegar, chilli sauce, garlic and kecap manis.

Peel and devein the prawns. Cut each prawn in half lengthways.

Cook the egg noodles in a large saucepan of boiling water for 2 minutes, or until tender, then drain thoroughly. Cool in a large bowl.

Add the dressing, prawns and remaining ingredients to the noodles and toss gently. Serve with the lime wedges.

singapore noodles

150 g (5 oz) dried rice vermicelli
oil, for cooking
250 g (9 oz) Chinese barbecued pork (char siu), cut into small pieces
250 g (9 oz) raw prawns (shrimp), peeled and cut into small pieces
2 tablespoons madras curry powder
2 garlic cloves, crushed
1 onion, thinly sliced
100 g (4 oz) shiitake mushrooms, thinly sliced
100 g (4 oz) green beans, thinly sliced on the diagonal
1 tablespoon soy sauce
4 spring onions (scallions), thinly sliced on the diagonal

serves 4–6

method Place the vermicelli in a large bowl, cover with boiling water and soak for 5 minutes. Drain well and spread out on a clean tea towel (dish towel) to dry.

Heat the wok until very hot, add 1 tablespoon of the oil and swirl it around to coat the side. Stir-fry the pork and the prawn pieces in batches over high heat. Remove from the wok.

Reheat the wok, add 2 tablespoons of the oil and stir-fry the curry powder and garlic for 1–2 minutes, or until fragrant. Add the onion and mushrooms, and stir-fry over medium heat for 2–3 minutes, or until the onion and mushrooms are soft.

Return the pork and prawns to the wok, add the beans and 2 teaspoons water, and toss to combine. Add the drained noodles, soy sauce and spring onion. Toss well and serve.

phad thai

250 g (9 oz) thick rice-stick noodles
2 tablespoons oil
3 garlic cloves, chopped
2 teaspoons chopped red chillies
150 g (5 oz) pork, thinly sliced
100 g (4 oz) raw prawns (shrimp), peeled and chopped
½ bunch garlic chives, snipped
2 tablespoons fish sauce
2 tablespoons lime juice
2 teaspoons soft brown sugar
2 eggs, beaten
90 g (3 oz/1 cup) bean sprouts
sprigs of coriander (cilantro)
3 tablespoons chopped roasted peanuts, plus extra, to serve (optional)
crisp fried onion and soft brown sugar, to serve (optional)

serves 4

method Soak the rice stick noodles in warm water for 10 minutes or until they are soft. Drain and set aside. Heat the oil to very hot in a wok or large frying pan, then add the garlic, chillies and pork and stir-fry for 2 minutes.

Add the prawn meat to the wok. Stir-fry for 3 minutes. Add the garlic chives and drained noodles, cover and cook for another minute. Add the fish sauce, lime juice, sugar and eggs to the wok. Toss well until heated through.

To serve, sprinkle with bean sprouts, coriander and chopped peanuts. Traditionally served with crisp fried onion, soft brown sugar and more chopped peanuts on the side.

chilli noodles with nuts

1½ tablespoons oil
1 tablespoon sesame oil
2–3 small red chillies, finely chopped
1 large onion, cut into thin wedges
4 garlic cloves, cut into paper-thin slices
1 red capsicum (pepper), cut into strips
1 green capsicum (pepper), cut into strips
2 large carrots, cut into thick matchsticks
100 g (4 oz) green beans
2 celery stalks, cut into matchsticks
2 teaspoons honey
500 g (1 lb 2 oz) hokkien (egg) noodles,
   gently separated
100 g (4 oz/⅔ cup) dry-roasted peanuts
100 g (4 oz/⅔ cup) honey-roasted
   cashew nuts
30 g (1 oz) snipped garlic chives, or 4 spring
   onions (scallions), chopped
sweet chilli sauce and sesame oil, to serve

serves 4

method   Heat the wok over low heat, add the oils and swirl them around to coat the side. When the oil is warm, add the chilli and heat until very hot.

Add the onion and garlic and stir-fry for 1 minute, or until the onion just softens. Add the capsicum, carrot and beans and stir-fry for 1 minute. Add the celery, honey and 1 tablespoon water and season with salt and pepper. Toss well, then cover and cook for 1–2 minutes, or until the vegetables are brightly coloured and just tender.

Add the noodles and nuts and toss well. Cook, covered, for 1–2 minutes, until the noodles are heated through. Stir in the garlic chives and serve, drizzled with the sweet chilli sauce and sesame oil.

sweet chilli chicken noodles

375 g (12 oz) hokkien (egg) noodles
4 boneless, skinless chicken thighs,
cut into small pieces
1–2 tablespoons sweet chilli sauce
2 teaspoons fish sauce
1 tablespoon oil
100 g (4 oz) baby sweet corn, halved
lengthways
150 g (5 oz) sugar snap peas,
topped and tailed
1 tablespoon lime juice

serves 4–6

method Place the noodles in a large bowl, cover with boiling water and gently break apart with a fork. Leave for 5 minutes, then drain.

Combine the chicken, sweet chilli sauce and fish sauce in a bowl.

Heat a wok or frying pan over high heat, add the oil and swirl to coat. Add the chicken and stir-fry for 3–5 minutes, or until cooked through. Then add the corn and sugar snap peas and stir-fry for 2 minutes. Add the noodles and lime juice and serve.

coriander noodles with tuna

3 tablespoons lime juice
2 tablespoons fish sauce
2 tablespoons sweet chilli sauce
2 teaspoons grated palm sugar (jaggery)
1 teaspoon sesame oil
1 garlic clove, finely chopped
1 tablespoon virgin olive oil
4 tuna steaks, at room temperature
200 g (7 oz) dried thin wheat noodles
6 spring onions (scallions), thinly sliced
2 very large handfuls coriander (cilantro)
   leaves, chopped, plus extra leaves, to garnish
lime wedges, to garnish

serves 4

method To make the dressing, mix together the lime juice, fish sauce, sweet chilli sauce, palm sugar, sesame oil and garlic.

Heat the olive oil in a chargrill pan. Add the tuna steaks and cook over high heat for 2 minutes each side, or until cooked to your liking. Transfer the steaks to a warm plate, cover and keep warm.

Place the noodles in a large saucepan of lightly salted, rapidly boiling water and return to the boil. Cook for 4 minutes, or until the noodles are tender. Drain well. Add half the dressing and half the spring onion and coriander to the noodles and gently toss together.

Either cut the tuna into even cubes or slice it. Arrange the noodles on plates and top with the tuna. Mix the remaining dressing with the spring onion and coriander and drizzle over the tuna. Garnish with lime wedges and coriander.

note *If you prefer, serve the tuna steaks whole. If serving whole, they would look better served with the noodles on the side.*

noodles with fried tofu

100 g (4 oz) deep-fried tofu puffs (see Note)
2 tablespoons oil
1 onion, sliced
1 red capsicum (pepper), cut into squares
3 garlic cloves, crushed
2 teaspoons grated fresh ginger
120 g (4 oz/¾ cup) small chunks
fresh pineapple
500 g (1 lb 2 oz) thin hokkien (egg) noodles,
separated
3 tablespoons pineapple juice
3 tablespoons hoisin sauce
1 very large handful roughly chopped
coriander (cilantro)

serves 4

method   Slice the tofu puffs into three, then cut each slice into two or three pieces.

Heat the wok until very hot, add the oil and stir-fry the onion and capsicum for 1–2 minutes, or until beginning to soften. Add the garlic and ginger, stir-fry for 1 minute, then add the tofu and stir-fry for 2 minutes.

Add the pineapple and noodles and toss until the mixture is combined and heated through. Add the pineapple juice, hoisin sauce and coriander and toss to combine. Serve immediately.

note   *Deep-fried tofu puffs are available from the refrigerated section in Asian grocery stores and some supermarkets. They have a very different texture to ordinary tofu.*

udon noodles

500 g (1 lb 2 oz) fresh udon noodles
1 tablespoon oil
6 spring onions (scallions), cut into
    short lengths
3 garlic cloves, crushed
1 tablespoon grated fresh ginger
2 carrots, cut into short lengths
150 g (5 oz) snow peas (mangetouts),
    cut in half on the diagonal
100 g (4 oz) bean sprouts
500 g (1 lb 2 oz) choy sum, cut into
    short lengths
2 tablespoons Japanese soy sauce
2 tablespoons mirin
2 tablespoons kecap manis (see Note,
    page 28)
2 sheets roasted nori (dried seaweed), cut
    into thin strips, plus extra, to garnish

serves 4

method   Bring a saucepan of water to the boil, add the noodles and cook for 5 minutes, or until tender and not clumped together. Drain and rinse under hot water.

Heat the oil in a wok until hot, then add the spring onion, garlic and ginger. Stir-fry over high heat for 1–2 minutes, or until soft. Add the carrot, snow peas and 1 tablespoon water, toss well, cover and cook for 1–2 minutes, or until the vegetables are just tender.

Add the noodles, bean sprouts, choy sum, soy sauce, mirin and kecap manis, then toss until the choy sum is wilted and coated with the sauce. Stir in the nori just before serving. Garnish with the extra nori.

vegetarian phad thai

400 g (14 oz) flat rice-stick noodles
2 tablespoons peanut oil
2 eggs, lightly beaten
1 onion, cut into thin wedges
2 garlic cloves, crushed
1 small red capsicum (pepper), thinly sliced
100 g (4 oz) fried tofu, cut into thin strips
6 spring onions (scallions), thinly sliced
2 very large handfuls coriander (cilantro)
leaves, chopped
3 tablespoons soy sauce
2 tablespoons lime juice
1 tablespoon soft brown sugar
2 teaspoons sambal oelek (South-East
Asian chilli paste)
90 g (3 oz/1 cup) bean sprouts
3 tablespoons chopped roasted
unsalted peanuts

serves 4

method   Cook the noodles in a saucepan of boiling water for 5–10 minutes, or until tender. Drain and set aside.

Heat a wok over high heat and add enough peanut oil to coat the bottom and side. When smoking, add the egg and swirl to form a thin omelette. Cook for 30 seconds, or until just set. Roll up, remove and thinly slice.

Heat the remaining oil in the wok. Add the onion, garlic and capsicum and cook over high heat for 2–3 minutes, or until the onion softens. Add the noodles, tossing well. Stir in the omelette, tofu, spring onion and half the coriander.

Pour in the combined soy sauce, lime juice, sugar and sambal oelek, then toss to coat the noodles. Sprinkle with the bean sprouts and top with roasted peanuts and the remaining coriander. Serve the phad thai immediately.

noodles with barbecued pork and greens

250 g (9 oz) fresh thick egg noodles
1 tablespoon oil
1 tablespoon sesame oil
250 g (9 oz) Chinese barbecued pork (char siu),
   cut into small cubes (see Note)
1 large onion, very thinly sliced
2 garlic cloves, finely chopped
400 g (14 oz) green vegetables (such as beans,
   broccoli, celery), cut into bite-sized pieces
2 tablespoons hoisin sauce
1 tablespoon kecap manis (see Note, page 28)
100 g (4 oz) snow peas (mangetouts)
3 baby bok choy (pak choy), leaves separated
230 g (8 oz) tin water chestnuts, sliced

serves 4

method   Two-thirds fill a pan with water and bring to the boil. Add the noodles and cook for about 3 minutes, or until just tender. Drain well.

Heat the wok until very hot, add the oils and swirl them around to coat the side. Stir-fry the pork over medium heat for 2 minutes, or until crisp. Drain on paper towels.

Reheat the wok, add the onion and garlic and stir-fry over very high heat for about 1 minute, until just softened. Add the vegetables and cook, tossing regularly, for 2 minutes, or until just softened. Stir in the hoisin sauce, kecap manis, snow peas, bok choy, water chestnuts and 1 tablespoon of water. Cook for 2 minutes, covered. Add the noodles and stir-fried pork, and toss gently to combine. Serve immediately.

note   *Chinese barbecued pork is also known as char siu. You can buy it at Chinese barbecue shops. You can use Asian greens instead of beans, broccoli and celery.*

noodles with chicken and fresh black beans

2 teaspoons salted black beans
oil, for cooking
2 teaspoons sesame oil
500 g (1 lb 2 oz) boneless, skinless chicken
thighs, thinly sliced
3 garlic cloves, very thinly sliced
4 spring onions (scallions), chopped
1 teaspoon sugar
1 red capsicum (pepper), sliced
100 g (4 oz) green beans, cut into
short pieces
300 g (11 oz) hokkien (egg) noodles
2 tablespoons oyster sauce
1 tablespoon soy sauce
coriander (cilantro) leaves, to garnish

serves 2–3

method Rinse the black beans in running water. Drain and roughly chop.

Heat the wok until very hot, add 1 tablespoon of oil and the sesame oil and swirl it around to coat the side. Stir-fry the chicken in three batches, until well browned, tossing regularly. Remove from the wok and set aside.

Reheat the wok, add 1 tablespoon of the oil and stir-fry the garlic and spring onion for 1 minute. Add the black beans, sugar, capsicum and beans and cook for 1 minute. Sprinkle with 2 tablespoons of water, cover and steam for 2 minutes.

Gently separate the noodles and add to the wok with the chicken, oyster sauce and soy sauce, and toss well. Cook, covered, for 2 minutes, or until the noodles are just softened. Serve immediately, garnished with the coriander.

curried chicken noodles

100 g (4 oz) dried rice vermicelli
oil, for cooking
500 g (1 lb 2 oz) boneless, skinless chicken
    breasts, cut into thin strips
2 garlic cloves, crushed
1 teaspoon grated fresh ginger
2 teaspoons Asian-style curry powder
1 red onion, sliced
1 red capsicum (pepper), thinly sliced
2 carrots, cut into matchsticks
2 zucchini (courgettes), cut into matchsticks
1 tablespoon soy sauce

serves 4

method   Place the vermicelli in a large bowl, cover with boiling water and soak for 5 minutes. Drain well and place on a tea towel (dish towel) to dry.

Heat the wok until very hot, add 1 tablespoon of the oil and swirl it around to coat the side. Stir-fry the chicken in several batches over high heat until browned and tender. Remove all the chicken and drain on paper towels.

Reheat the wok, add 1 tablespoon of the oil and stir-fry the garlic, ginger, curry powder and onion for 1–2 minutes, or until fragrant. Add the capsicum, carrot and zucchini to the wok, and stir-fry until well coated in the spices. Add 1 tablespoon water and stir-fry for 1 minute.

Add the drained noodles and chicken to the wok. Add the soy sauce and toss well. Season with salt before serving.

kedgeree

600 g (1 lb 5 oz) smoked haddock
50 g (2 oz) butter
1 onion, finely chopped
2 teaspoons curry powder
1 teaspoon ground cumin
1 teaspoon ground coriander
2 teaspoons seeded and finely
sliced green chilli
200 g (7 oz/1 cup) basmati rice
660 ml (23 fl oz) chicken or fish stock
1 cinnamon stick
4 tablespoons cream
2 hard-boiled eggs, finely chopped
2 tablespoons chopped parsley
2 tablespoons chopped coriander (cilantro)

serves 4

method Poach the haddock in a large shallow frying pan, skin side up: cover with boiling water and simmer very gently for about 10 minutes. The fish is cooked when the flesh can be flaked easily with a fork. Drain and pat dry with paper towels. Remove the skin and flake into bite-size chunks.

Heat the butter in a large saucepan and add the onion. Cook until golden, then add the curry powder, cumin, coriander and chilli. Cook, stirring, for 1 minute. Add the rice, stir well, then pour in the stock and add the cinnamon stick. Cover tightly and simmer over gentle heat for about 12 minutes, or until the rice is tender.

Remove the cinnamon stick and gently stir in the haddock. Fold through the cream, chopped egg and the herbs. Season and serve immediately.

chinese fried rice

2 tablespoons peanut oil
2 eggs, lightly beaten and seasoned
2 teaspoons lard (optional)
1 onion, cut into wedges
250 g (9 oz) ham, cut into thin strips
750 g (1 lb 10 oz/4 cups) cold cooked rice
   (see Note)
3 tablespoons frozen peas
2 tablespoons soy sauce
4 spring onions (scallions), cut into
   short lengths
250 g (9 oz) cooked small prawns (shrimp),
   peeled

serves 4

method Heat 1 tablespoon of the peanut oil in a wok or large frying pan and add the eggs, pulling the set egg towards the centre and tilting the wok to let the unset egg run to the edge. When it is almost set, break up the egg into large pieces to resemble scrambled eggs. Transfer to a plate.

Heat the remaining oil and lard in the wok, swirling to coat the base and side. Stir-fry the onion over high heat until softened. Add the ham and stir-fry for 1 minute. Add the rice and peas and stir-fry for 3 minutes, or until the rice is heated through. Add the eggs, soy sauce, spring onion and prawns. Heat through and serve.

notes *Rice should be refrigerated overnight before making fried rice to let the grains separate and dry out. You can include Chinese barbecued pork (char siu), Chinese sausage (lap cheong) or bacon instead of ham.*

44

fried rice with coriander and basil

2 tablespoons oil
2.5 cm (1 inch) piece pork fat, chopped
4 garlic cloves, chopped
2 tablespoons grated fresh ginger
2 teaspoons chopped red chillies
2 boneless, skinless chicken thighs, diced
100 g (4 oz) pork loin, diced
470 g (1 lb 1 oz/2⅓ cups) cold cooked
jasmine rice (see Note)
1 tablespoon fish sauce
2 teaspoons light soy sauce
2 spring onions (scallions), chopped
1 very large handful Thai basil leaves, chopped
1 very large handful coriander (cilantro)
leaves, chopped

serves 4

method Heat the oil to very hot in a wok. Stir-fry the pork fat, garlic, ginger and chilli for 2 minutes.

Add the diced chicken and pork to the wok and stir-fry for 3 minutes, or until the meat changes colour. Break up any lumps in the rice; add to the wok and toss well to warm through. Add the sauces and toss through with the spring onions and herbs.

note *Rice should be refrigerated overnight before making fried rice to let the grains dry out and separate.*

meat

spicy lamb soup

2 large onions, roughly chopped
3 red chillies, seeded and chopped
   (or 2 teaspoons dried chilli)
3–4 garlic cloves
2.5 cm (1 inch) piece fresh ginger, peeled
   and chopped
5 cm (2 inch) lemongrass, white part only,
   finely chopped
½ teaspoon ground cardamom
2 teaspoons ground cumin
½ teaspoon ground cinnamon
1 teaspoon ground turmeric
2 tablespoons peanut oil
1.5 kg (3 lb 5 oz) lamb neck chops
2–3 tablespoons vindaloo paste
600 ml (21 fl oz) coconut cream
3 tablespoons soft brown sugar
2–3 tablespoons lime juice
4 makrut (kaffir lime) leaves

serves 4–6

method Put the onion, chilli, garlic, ginger, 1 teaspoon ground black pepper, lemongrass, cardamom, cumin, cinnamon and turmeric in a food processor and process to a paste. Heat half the oil in a large frying pan and brown the chops in batches. Drain on paper towels.

Add the remaining oil to the pan and cook the spice and vindaloo pastes for 2–3 minutes. Add the lamb chops and 1.75 litres (7 cups) water, cover and bring to the boil. Reduce the heat and simmer, covered, for 1 hour. Remove the chops from the pan and stir in the coconut cream. Remove the meat from the bones, shred and return to the pan.

Add the sugar, lime juice and makrut leaves. Simmer, uncovered, over low heat for 20–25 minutes, until slightly thickened.

tandoori lamb salad

250 g (9 oz/1 cup) low-fat plain yoghurt
2 garlic cloves, crushed
2 teaspoons grated fresh ginger
2 teaspoons ground turmeric
2 teaspoons garam masala
¼ teaspoon paprika
2 teaspoons ground coriander
red food colouring (optional)
500 g (1 lb 2 oz) lean lamb loin fillets
4 tablespoons lemon juice
1½ teaspoons chopped coriander (cilantro)
1 teaspoon chopped mint
150 g (5 oz) mixed salad leaves
1 large mango, cut into strips
2 Lebanese (short) cucumbers, cut into matchsticks

serves 4

method Mix the yoghurt, garlic, ginger and spices in a bowl, add a little colouring and toss with the lamb to thoroughly coat. Cover and refrigerate overnight.

Grill the lamb on a foil-lined baking tray under high heat for 7 minutes each side, or until the marinade starts to brown. Set aside for 5 minutes before serving.

Mix the lemon juice, coriander and mint, then season. Toss with the salad leaves, mango and cucumber, then arrange on plates. Slice the lamb and serve over the salad.

thai beef salad

3 garlic cloves, finely chopped
4 coriander (cilantro) roots, finely chopped
3 tablespoons oil
400 g (14 oz) piece rump or sirloin steak
1 small soft-leaved lettuce, leaves separated
200 g (7 oz) cherry tomatoes, halved
1 Lebanese (short) cucumber, thickly sliced
4 spring onions (scallions), chopped
1 very large handful coriander (cilantro) leaves

dressing

2 tablespoons fish sauce
2 tablespoons lime juice
1 tablespoon soy sauce
2 teaspoons chopped red chillies
2 teaspoons soft brown sugar

serves 4

method   Finely grind the chopped garlic, coriander roots, $1/2$ teaspoon black pepper and 2 tablespoons of the oil in a mortar and pestle, food processor or blender. Spread evenly over the steak.

Heat the remaining oil in a heavy-based frying pan or wok over high heat. Add the steak to the pan and cook for about 4 minutes each side, turning once only during the cooking time. Remove and allow to cool.

Meanwhile, combine the lettuce, cherry tomatoes, cucumber and spring onion on a serving plate.

To make the dressing, stir together the fish sauce, lime juice, soy sauce, chillies and brown sugar until the sugar has dissolved.

Cut the steak into thin strips. Arrange over the salad and toss together very gently. Drizzle with the dressing and scatter the coriander over the top. Serve immediately.

hint   *Don't overcook the steak—it should be pink and, therefore, succulent and tender.*

hoisin pork with stir-fried greens

250 g (9 oz/1¼ cups) jasmine rice
500 g (1 lb 2 oz) pork fillet, thinly sliced
1 tablespoon caster (superfine) sugar
2 tablespoons oil
125 ml (4 fl oz/½ cup) white wine vinegar
250 ml (9 fl oz/1 cup) hoisin sauce
2 tablespoons stem ginger in syrup,
chopped (see Note)
1.25 kg (2 lb 12 oz) mixed Asian greens, such as
bok choy (pak choy), choy sum or spinach

serves 4

method   Rinse the rice and place in a large saucepan. Add 435 ml (15 fl oz/1¾ cups) water and bring to the boil. Cover, reduce the heat to very low and cook for 10 minutes. Remove from the heat and leave to stand, covered, for 10 minutes.

Meanwhile, place the pork in a bowl and sprinkle with the sugar. Toss to coat. Heat a wok over high heat, add 1 tablespoon of oil and swirl to coat. Add the pork in batches and stir-fry for 3 minutes, or until brown. Remove all the pork from the wok. Add the vinegar to the wok and boil for 3–5 minutes, or until reduced by two-thirds. Reduce the heat, add the hoisin sauce and 1 tablespoon ginger, and simmer for 5 minutes.

Reheat the wok over high heat, add the remaining oil and swirl to coat. Add the greens and stir-fry for 3 minutes, until crisp and cooked. Stir the remaining ginger through the rice, then press into four round teacups or small Asian bowls, smoothing the surface. Unmould the rice onto four serving plates, arrange the pork and greens on the side and drizzle the sauce over the top.

note   *Stem ginger is available from Asian food stores. Use glacé (candied) ginger if it is unavailable.*

honey and black pepper beef

oil, for cooking
500 g (1 lb 2 oz) round steak, cut into
    thin strips
2 garlic cloves, crushed
1 onion, sliced
300 g (11 oz) sugar snap peas
2 tablespoons honey
2 teaspoons soy sauce
2 tablespoons oyster sauce

serves 4

method   Heat the wok until very hot, add 1 tablespoon of the oil and swirl it around to coat the side. Stir-fry the beef in batches over high heat. Remove and drain on paper towels.

Reheat the wok, add 1 tablespoon of the oil and stir-fry the garlic, onion and peas until softened. Remove from the wok and set aside.

Add the honey, soy sauce, oyster sauce and 3 teaspoons cracked black pepper to the wok. Bring to the boil, then reduce the heat and simmer for 3–4 minutes, or until the sauce thickens slightly.

Increase the heat, return the meat and vegetables to the wok, and toss for 2–3 minutes, or until well combined and heated through.

barbecued pork and broccoli

1 tablespoon oil
1 large onion, thinly sliced
2 carrots, cut into matchsticks
200 g (7 oz) broccoli, cut into bite-sized florets
6 spring onions (scallions), diagonally sliced
1 tablespoon finely chopped fresh ginger
3 garlic cloves, finely chopped
400 g (14 oz) Chinese barbecued pork
(char siu), thinly sliced (see Note)
2 tablespoons soy sauce
2 tablespoons mirin
180 g (6 oz/2 cups) bean sprouts

serves 4–6

method   Heat the wok until very hot, add the oil and swirl it around to coat the side. Stir-fry the onion over medium heat for 3–4 minutes, or until slightly softened. Add the carrot, broccoli, spring onion, ginger and garlic, and stir-fry for 4–5 minutes.

Increase the heat to high and add the barbecued pork. Toss constantly until the pork is well mixed with the vegetables and heated through. Add the soy sauce and mirin, and toss until the ingredients are well coated. (The wok should be hot enough that the sauce reduces a little to form a glaze-like consistency.) Add the bean sprouts and season well with salt and pepper. Serve immediately.

note   *Chinese barbecued pork is available from Asian stores.*

tonkatsu

500 g (1 lb 2 oz) pork loin
60 g (2 oz/½ cup) plain (all-purpose) flour
6 egg yolks, beaten with 2 tablespoons water
120 g (4 oz/2 cups) Japanese dried
   breadcrumbs (panko)
2 spring onions (scallions)
pickled ginger and pickled daikon
90 g (3 oz/2 cups) finely shredded Chinese
   or savoy cabbage
1 sheet nori (dried seaweed)
375 ml (13 fl oz/1½ cups) oil
250 ml (9 fl oz/1 cup) tonkatsu sauce

serves 4

method Cut the pork into 8 thin slices. Sprinkle with salt and pepper and lightly coat with flour.

Dip the pork in the egg and then the breadcrumbs, pressing the crumbs on with your fingertips for an even coating. Arrange in a single layer on a plate and refrigerate, uncovered, for at least 2 hours.

To prepare the garnishes, peel away the outside layers of the spring onions, then slice the stems very finely and place in a bowl of cold water until serving time. Slice the ginger and daikon and set aside with the shredded cabbage. Using a sharp knife, shred the nori very finely and then break into strips about 4 cm (1½ inches) long.

Heat the oil in a heavy-based frying pan. Cook 2–3 pork steaks at a time until golden brown on both sides, then drain on kitchen towels. Slice the pork into strips and reassemble into the original steak shape. Top each one with a few nori strips. Serve with the tonkatsu sauce, shredded cabbage, drained spring onions, pickled ginger, daikon and steamed rice.

indian spiced lamb

3 tablespoons oil
2 tablespoons madras curry powder,
or to taste
4 lamb fillets
1 tablespoon brinjal pickle (see Notes)
250 g (9 oz/1 cup) Greek-style yoghurt
350 g (12 oz/1¾ cups) couscous
½ red capsicum (pepper), diced
4 spring onions (scallions), sliced

serves 4–6

method Mix together 2 tablespoons oil and the curry powder. Place the lamb in a non-metallic dish and brush the curry oil over it. Cover and marinate for 30 minutes. Preheat the oven to 180°C (350°F/Gas 4).

Place the brinjal pickle and yoghurt in a bowl and mix together well. Add 2 tablespoons water and set aside. Heat the remaining oil in a frying pan, add the lamb and cook for 2–3 minutes on each side to seal. Transfer to an ovenproof dish and cook in the oven for 10–12 minutes. Remove from the oven and rest, covered, for 5 minutes, then carve into slices.

Meanwhile, place the couscous in a bowl. Season with salt and cover with 455 ml (16 fl oz) boiling water. Leave for 5 minutes, or until all the liquid has been absorbed. Fluff the couscous with a fork to separate the grains. Cool, then add the capsicum, spring onion and half of the yoghurt mixture. Serve the lamb slices on a bed of couscous. Drizzle the remaining yoghurt mixture over the top.

notes *Brinjal pickle is made from eggplant (aubergine) and is widely available. If you can't find it, try mango chutney. With the couscous you can use orange juice instead of water, and nuts and sultanas (golden raisins) instead of capsicums and onions.*

sweet and sour pork

500 g (1 lb 2 oz) pork fillet, cut into thick slices
2 tablespoons cornflour (cornstarch)
1 tablespoon sherry
1 tablespoon soy sauce
1 tablespoon sugar
oil, for cooking
1 large onion, thinly sliced
1 green capsicum (pepper), cut into squares
2 small carrots, thinly sliced
1 small Lebanese (short) cucumber, seeded
    and chopped
5 spring onions (scallions), cut into short
    lengths
440 g (15 oz) tin pineapple pieces in natural
    juice, drained and juice reserved
3 tablespoons white vinegar

serves 4

method Place the pork in a shallow glass or ceramic bowl. Combine the cornflour with the sherry, soy sauce and half the sugar, and pour into the bowl. Cover and refrigerate for 30 minutes.

Drain the pork, reserving the marinade. Heat the wok until very hot, add 2 tablespoons of the oil and swirl to coat the side. Stir-fry half the pork over high heat for 4–5 minutes, or until the pork is golden brown and just cooked. Remove from the wok, add more oil if necessary and repeat with the rest of the pork. Remove all the pork from the wok.

Reheat the wok, add 1 tablespoon of the oil and stir-fry the onion over high heat for 3–4 minutes, or until slightly softened. Add the capsicum and carrot, and cook for 3–4 minutes, or until tender. Stir in the marinade, cucumber, spring onion, pineapple, vinegar, 1/2 teaspoon salt, the remaining sugar and 4 tablespoons of the pineapple juice.

Bring to the boil and simmer for 2–3 minutes, or until the sauce has thickened slightly. Return all of the pork to the wok and toss to heat through.

100 EASY RECIPES ASIAN

mongolian lamb

oil, for cooking
500 g (1 lb 2 oz) lamb backstrap (tender eye of
the lamb loin), cut into thin strips
2 garlic cloves, crushed
4 spring onions (scallions), thickly sliced
2 tablespoons soy sauce
4 tablespoons dry sherry
2 tablespoons sweet chilli sauce
2 teaspoons sesame seeds, toasted

serves 4

method Heat the wok until very hot, add 1 tablespoon of the oil and swirl it around to coat the side. Stir-fry the lamb strips in batches over high heat. Remove all the lamb from the wok.

Reheat the wok, add 1 tablespoon of oil and stir-fry the garlic and spring onion for 2 minutes. Remove from the wok and set aside. Add the soy sauce, sherry and sweet chilli sauce to the wok. Bring to the boil, reduce the heat and simmer for 3–4 minutes, or until the sauce thickens slightly.

Return the meat, with any juices, and the garlic and spring onion to the wok, and toss to coat. Serve sprinkled with the toasted sesame seeds.

teppan yaki

350 g (12 oz) beef fillet, partially frozen
4 small slender eggplants (aubergines)
100 g (4 oz) fresh shiitake mushrooms
100 g (4 oz) baby green beans
6 yellow or green baby (pattypan) squash
1 red or green capsicum (pepper), seeded
6 spring onions (scallions)
200 g (7 oz) tinned bamboo shoots, drained
3 tablespoons vegetable oil
soy and ginger dipping sauce

serves 4

method Slice the steak very thinly. Mark a large cross on each slice of meat. Place the slices in a single layer and season well.

Trim the ends from the eggplants and cut the flesh into long, very thin diagonal slices. Trim any tough stalks from the mushrooms and top and tail the beans. Quarter or halve the squash, depending on the size. Cut the capsicum into thin strips and slice the spring onions into long pieces. Trim the bamboo shoot slices to a similar size. Arrange the vegetables in separate bundles.

Heat an electric grill or electric frying pan until very hot and then lightly brush it with the oil. Quickly fry about a quarter of the meat, searing on both sides, and then move it over to the edge of the pan. Add about a quarter of the vegetables to the grill or pan and quickly stir-fry, adding a little more oil as needed. Serve a small portion of the meat and vegetables to each guest with sauces for dipping.

beef and spinach curry

2 tablespoons oil
1 onion, finely chopped
2 garlic cloves, finely chopped
2 teaspoons ground cumin
2 teaspoons ground coriander
2 teaspoons paprika
1 teaspoon garam masala
1 teaspoon turmeric
½ teaspoon finely chopped red chilli
1 teaspoon finely chopped green chilli
2 teaspoons grated fresh ginger
500 g (1 lb 2 oz) lean minced (ground) beef
or lamb
1 tomato, chopped
250 ml (9 fl oz/1 cup) beef stock or water
500 g (1 lb 2 oz) English spinach, chopped
200 g (7 oz) plain yoghurt

serves 4

method Heat 1 tablespoon of the oil in a large saucepan and cook the onion over medium heat until golden brown. Add the garlic, cumin, coriander, paprika, garam masala, turmeric, red and green chilli and the grated ginger and stir for 1 minute. Remove and set aside.

Heat the remaining oil in the pan and brown the meat over high heat, breaking up any lumps with a fork or wooden spoon. Return the onion mixture to the pan and add the tomato and stock or water.

Bring the mixture to the boil and then reduce the heat and simmer for about 1 hour. Season with salt, to taste. Meanwhile, cook the spinach briefly. Just before serving, add the spinach to the mixture and stir in the yoghurt.

note *If possible, make the meat mixture in advance and refrigerate overnight for the flavours to develop.*

beef rendang

2 onions, roughly chopped
2 garlic cloves, crushed
400 ml (14 fl oz) coconut milk
2 teaspoons ground coriander seeds
½ teaspoon ground fennel seeds
2 teaspoons ground cumin seeds
¼ teaspoon ground cloves
1.5 kg (3 lb 5 oz) chuck steak, cubed
4–6 small red chillies, chopped
1 tablespoon lemon juice
1 lemongrass stem, white part only, bruised,
  cut lengthways
2 teaspoons grated palm sugar (jaggery)
  or soft brown sugar

serves 6

method Mix the onion and garlic in a food processor until smooth, adding water, if necessary.

Put the coconut milk in a large saucepan and bring to the boil. Reduce the heat to medium and cook, stirring occasionally, for 15 minutes, or until reduced by half and the oil has separated. Do not allow to brown.

Add the coriander, fennel, cumin and cloves to the pan and stir for 1 minute. Add the meat and cook for 2 minutes, or until it changes colour. Add the onion mixture, chilli, lemon juice, lemongrass and sugar. Cook, covered, over medium heat for 2 hours, or until the liquid has reduced and the mixture has thickened. Stir frequently to prevent sticking.

Uncover and cook until the oil from the coconut milk begins to emerge again, giving the curry colour and flavour. Be careful not to burn. The curry is cooked when it is brown and dry.

madras beef curry

1 tablespoon oil
2 onions, finely chopped
3 garlic cloves, finely chopped
1 tablespoon grated fresh ginger
4 tablespoons madras curry paste
1 kg (2 lb 4 oz) chuck steak, diced
3 tablespoons tomato paste
(concentrated purée)
250 ml (9 fl oz/1 cup) beef stock
6 new potatoes, halved
155 g (5 oz/1 cup) frozen peas

serves 6

method Preheat the oven to 180°C (350°F/Gas 4). Heat the oil in a large heavy-based 3 litre (12 cup) flameproof casserole. Cook the onion over medium heat for 4–5 minutes. Add the garlic and ginger and cook, stirring, for 5 minutes, or until the onion is lightly golden, taking care not to burn it.

Add the curry paste and cook, stirring, for 2 minutes, or until fragrant. Increase the heat to high, add the meat and stir constantly for 2–3 minutes, or until the meat is well coated. Add the tomato paste and stock and stir well.

Bake, covered, for 50 minutes, stirring 2–3 times during cooking, and add a little water if necessary. Reduce the oven to 160°C (315°F/Gas 2–3). Add the potato and cook for 30 minutes, then add the peas and cook for another 10 minutes, or until the potato is tender.

beef and pineapple curry

2 tablespoons peanut oil
500 g (1 lb 2 oz) rump steak, thinly sliced
  across the grain
2 tablespoons penang curry paste
2 onions, cut into thin wedges
2 garlic cloves, crushed
500 ml (17 fl oz/2 cups) tin coconut milk
8 makrut (kaffir lime) leaves
320 g (11 oz/2 cups) chopped fresh
  pineapple
2 teaspoons soft brown sugar
2 tablespoons lime juice
1 tablespoon fish sauce
3 tablespoons chopped coriander
  (cilantro) leaves

serves 4

method   Heat a wok over high heat, add half the oil and swirl to coat the sides. Add the beef in batches and stir-fry for 2 minutes, or until browned. Remove.

Heat the remaining oil in the wok over high heat, add the curry paste and cook for 1 minute, or until fragrant. Add the onion and garlic and cook for 1–2 minutes, or until the onion is soft.

Return the beef to the wok, add the coconut milk, makrut leaves and pineapple and bring to the boil, then reduce the heat and simmer for 5 minutes, or until the beef is just cooked. Stir in the remaining ingredients just before serving.

kashmir lamb with spinach

2 tablespoons oil
750 g (1 lb 10 oz) diced leg of lamb
2 large onions, chopped
3 garlic cloves, crushed
5 cm (2 inch) piece fresh ginger, grated
2 teaspoons ground cumin
2 teaspoons ground coriander
2 teaspoons turmeric
¼ teaspoon ground cardamom
¼ teaspoon ground cloves
3 bay leaves
375 ml (13 fl oz/1½ cups) chicken stock
125 ml (4 fl oz/½ cup) cream
2 bunches English spinach leaves,
washed and chopped

serves 4

method Heat the oil in a heavy-based pan and brown the lamb in batches. Remove from the pan. Add the onion, garlic and ginger and cook for 3 minutes, stirring regularly. Add the cumin, coriander, turmeric, cardamom and cloves and cook, stirring, for 1–2 minutes, or until fragrant. Return the lamb to the pan with any juices. Add the bay leaves and stock.

Bring to the boil and then reduce the heat, stir well, cover and simmer for 35 minutes. Add the cream and cook, covered, for a further 20 minutes or until the lamb is very tender. Add the spinach and cook until it has softened. Season to taste before serving.

note *Curry is best cooked a day in advance and refrigerated. Do not add the spinach until reheating.*

bombay lamb curry

1.5 kg (3 lb 5 oz) leg of lamb, boned
   (ask your butcher to do this)
2 tablespoons ghee or oil
2 onions, finely chopped
2 garlic cloves, crushed
2 small green chillies, finely chopped
5 cm (2 inch) piece fresh ginger, grated
1½ teaspoons turmeric
2 teaspoons ground cumin
3 teaspoons ground coriander
½–1 teaspoon chilli powder
425 g (15 oz) tin chopped tomatoes
2 tablespoons coconut cream

serves 4–6

method Cut the meat into cubes, removing any skin and fat. You will have about 1 kg (2 lb 4 oz) meat remaining. Heat the ghee or oil in a large heavy-based frying pan over medium–high heat. Add the onion and cook, stirring frequently, for 10 minutes until golden brown. Add the garlic, chilli and ginger and stir for a further 2 minutes, taking care not to burn them.

Mix together the turmeric, cumin, coriander and chilli powder. Stir to a smooth paste with 2 tablespoons water and add to the frying pan. Stir for 2 minutes, taking care not to burn.

Add the meat a handful at a time, stirring to coat with spices. It is important to make sure all the meat is well-coated and browned.

Add 1–1½ teaspoons salt to taste and stir in the tomatoes. Bring to the boil, cover and reduce the heat to low. Simmer for 30 minutes and then stir in the coconut cream. Simmer for another 30 minutes, or until the lamb is tender.

storage *Keep covered and refrigerated for up to 3 days. The flavour of curry improves if it is kept for at least a day.*

pork vindaloo

3 tablespoons oil
1 kg (2 lb 4 oz) pork fillets, cubed
2 onions, finely chopped
4 garlic cloves, finely chopped
1 tablespoon finely chopped fresh ginger
1 tablespoon garam masala
2 teaspoons brown mustard seeds
4 tablespoons vindaloo paste

serves 4

method Heat the oil in a frying pan, add the meat in small batches and brown over medium heat for 5–7 minutes. Remove all the meat from the pan.

Add the onion, garlic, ginger, garam masala and brown mustard seeds to the pan and cook, stirring, for 5 minutes, or until the onion is soft.

Return all the meat to the pan, add the vindaloo paste and cook, stirring, for 2 minutes. Add 625 ml (22 fl oz/2$^1/_2$ cups) water and bring to the boil. Reduce the heat and simmer, covered, for 1$^1/_2$ hours, or until the meat is tender.

massaman beef curry

1 tablespoon tamarind pulp
2 tablespoons oil
750 g (1 lb 10 oz) lean stewing beef, cubed
500 ml (17 fl oz/2 cups) coconut milk
4 cardamom pods, bruised
500 ml (17 fl oz/2 cups) coconut cream
2–3 tablespoons massaman curry paste
8 baby onions, peeled
8 new potatoes, peeled
2 tablespoons fish sauce
2 tablespoons palm sugar (jaggery)
90 g (3 oz/²/₃ cup) unsalted peanuts, roasted
    and ground
coriander (cilantro) leaves, to garnish

serves 4

method   Place the tamarind pulp and 125 ml (4 fl oz/¹/₂ cup) boiling water in a bowl and set aside to cool. When cool, mash the pulp to dissolve in the water, then strain and reserve the liquid. Discard the pulp.

Heat the oil in a wok or a large saucepan and cook the beef in batches over high heat for 5 minutes, or until browned. Reduce the heat and add the coconut milk and cardamom, and simmer for 1 hour, or until the beef is tender. Remove and reserve the beef. Strain and reserve the cooking liquid, discarding the solids.

Heat the coconut cream in the wok and stir in the curry paste. Cook for 5 minutes, or until the oil starts to separate from the cream.

Add the baby onions, potatoes, fish sauce, palm sugar, peanuts, beef mixture, reserved cooking liquid and tamarind water, and simmer for 25–30 minutes. Garnish with coriander leaves to serve.

lamb kofta curry

500 g (1 lb 2 oz) minced (ground) lean lamb
1 onion, finely chopped
1 garlic clove, finely chopped
1 teaspoon grated fresh ginger
1 small fresh chilli, finely chopped
1 teaspoon garam masala
1 teaspoon ground coriander
3 tablespoons ground almonds
2 tablespoons coriander (cilantro) leaves
plain yoghurt, to serve

sauce

2 teaspoons oil
1 onion, finely chopped
3 tablespoons korma curry paste
400 g (14 oz) tin chopped tomatoes
125 g (5 oz/½ cup) low-fat yoghurt
1 teaspoon lemon juice

serves 4

method   Combine the lamb, onion, garlic, ginger, chilli, garam masala, ground coriander, ground almonds and 1 teaspoon salt in a bowl. Shape into walnut-sized balls with your hands.

Heat a large non-stick frying pan and cook the koftas in batches until brown on both sides—they don't have to be cooked all the way through.

To make the sauce, heat the oil in a frying pan over low heat. Add the onion and cook for 6–8 minutes, or until soft and golden. Add the curry paste and cook until fragrant. Add the tomatoes and simmer for 5 minutes. Stir in the yoghurt, a tablespoon at a time, and then the lemon juice.

Put the koftas in the tomato. Cook, covered, over low heat for 20 minutes. Garnish with the coriander leaves and serve with the yoghurt.

rogan josh

1 kg (2 lb 4 oz) leg of lamb, boned
1 tablespoon ghee or oil
2 onions, chopped
125 g (5 oz/½ cup) plain yoghurt
1 teaspoon chilli powder
1 tablespoon ground coriander
2 teaspoons ground cumin
1 teaspoon ground cardamom
½ teaspoon ground cloves
1 teaspoon ground turmeric
3 garlic cloves, crushed
1 tablespoon grated fresh ginger
400 g (14 oz) tin chopped tomatoes
3 tablespoons slivered almonds
1 teaspoon garam masala
chopped coriander (cilantro) leaves,
    to garnish

serves 4–6

method Trim the lamb of any excess fat or sinew and cut into small cubes. Heat the ghee or oil in a large saucepan, add the onion and cook, stirring, for 5 minutes, or until soft. Stir in the yoghurt, chilli powder, ground coriander, cumin, cardamom, cloves, turmeric, garlic and ginger. Add the tomato and 1 teaspoon salt and simmer for 5 minutes.

Add the lamb and stir until coated. Cover and cook over low heat, stirring occasionally, for 1–1½ hours, or until the lamb is tender. Uncover and simmer until the liquid thickens.

Meanwhile, toast the almonds in a dry frying pan over medium heat for 3–4 minutes, shaking the pan gently, until the nuts are golden brown. Remove from the pan at once to prevent them from burning.

Add the garam masala to the curry and mix through well. Sprinkle the slivered almonds and coriander leaves over the top and serve.

japanese pork schnitzel curry

1 tablespoon oil
1 onion, cut into thin wedges
2 large carrots, diced
1 large potato, diced
60 g (2 oz) Japanese curry paste block,
broken into small pieces (see Note)
plain (all-purpose) flour, for coating
4 x 120 g (4 oz) pork schnitzels,
pounded until thin
2 eggs, lightly beaten
150 g (5 oz/2½ cups) Japanese
breadcrumbs (panko)
oil, for deep-frying
pickled ginger, pickled daikon, umeboshi
(pickled baby plums) and crisp-fried onion,
to garnish

serves 4

method Heat the oil in a saucepan, add the onion, carrot and potato and cook over medium heat for 10 minutes, or until starting to brown. Add 500 ml (17 fl oz/2 cups) water and the curry paste and stir until the curry paste dissolves and the sauce has a smooth consistency. Reduce the heat and simmer for 10 minutes, or until the vegetables are cooked through.

Season the flour well with salt and pepper. Dip each schnitzel into the flour, shake off any excess and dip into the beaten egg, allowing any excess to drip off. Coat with the Japanese breadcrumbs by pressing each side of the schnitzel firmly into the crumbs on a plate.

Fill a deep heavy-based saucepan one-third full of oil and heat to 180°C (350°F), until a cube of bread browns in 15 seconds. Cook the schnitzels, one at a time, turning once or twice, for 5 minutes, until golden brown all over and cooked through. Drain on crumpled paper towels.

Slice each schnitzel and then arrange in the original shape over rice. Ladle the curry sauce over the schnitzels. Garnish with fried onions and serve with the pickles on the side.

note *Japanese curry comes in a solid block or in powder form and is available in Asian supermarkets. It varies from mild to very hot.*

poultry

baby corn and chicken soup

150 g (5 oz) whole baby corn (see Note)
1 tablespoon oil
2 lemongrass stems, white part only,
    very thinly sliced
2 tablespoons grated fresh ginger
6 spring onions (scallions), chopped
1 red chilli, finely chopped
1 litre (35 fl oz/4 cups) chicken stock
375 ml (13 fl oz/1½ cups) coconut milk
250 g (9 oz) boneless, skinless chicken breasts,
    thinly sliced
135 g (4 oz) creamed corn
1 tablespoon soy sauce
2 tablespoons finely snipped chives, to serve
1 red chilli, thinly sliced, to serve

serves 4

method   Cut the baby corn in half or quarters lengthways, depending on their size.

Heat the oil in a saucepan over medium heat and cook the lemongrass, ginger, spring onion and chilli for 1 minute, stirring continuously. Add the stock and coconut milk and bring to the boil—do not cover or the coconut milk will curdle.

Add the corn, chicken and creamed corn and simmer for 8 minutes, or until the corn and chicken are just tender. Add the soy sauce, season well and serve garnished with the chives and chilli.

note   *Tinned baby corn can be substituted for fresh corn. Add during the last 2 minutes of cooking.*

mulligatawny soup

30 g (1 oz) butter
375 g (13 oz) chicken thigh cutlets, skin and fat removed
1 large onion, finely chopped
1 apple, peeled, cored and diced
1 tablespoon curry paste
2 tablespoons plain (all-purpose) flour
750 ml (26 fl oz/3 cups) chicken stock
3 tablespoons basmati rice
1 tablespoon chutney
1 tablespoon lemon juice
3 tablespoons cream

serves 4

method   Heat the butter in a large heavy-based saucepan and brown the chicken for 5 minutes, then remove from the pan. Add the onion, apple and curry paste to the pan. Cook for 5 minutes, or until the onion is soft. Stir in the flour, cook for another 2 minutes, then add half the stock. Stir until the mixture boils and thickens.

Return the chicken to the pan with the remaining stock. Stir until boiling, reduce the heat, cover and simmer for 45 minutes. Add the rice and cook for a further 15 minutes.

Remove the chicken, dice the meat finely and return to the pan. Add the chutney, lemon juice, cream and salt and pepper to taste.

duck and indian spiced rice salad

dressing

4 tablespoons oil
1 teaspoon walnut oil
1 teaspoon grated orange zest
1 tablespoon orange juice
1 tablespoon finely chopped preserved ginger
1 teaspoon sambal oelek (South-East
  Asian chilli paste)
1 teaspoon white wine vinegar

100 g (4 oz/½ cup) wild rice
oil, for cooking
50 g (2 oz/½ cup) pecans
½ teaspoon ground cumin
½ teaspoon garam masala
¼ teaspoon cayenne pepper
75 g (3 oz) long-grain white rice
1 celery stalk, finely sliced
20 yellow pear tomatoes, cut in half
  lengthways
20 g (1 oz) baby English spinach leaves
4 spring onions (scallions), thinly sliced
450 g (1 lb) Chinese barbecued duck, with skin,
  cut into pieces (see Note)
strips of orange zest, to garnish

serves 4–6

method To make the dressing, mix the ingredients together thoroughly. Season with some salt and freshly ground black pepper.

Rinse the wild rice under cold water and add to 300 ml (11 fl oz) simmering water. Cook, covered, for 45 minutes, or until the grains puff open. Drain off any excess water.

Meanwhile, heat 2 teaspoons oil in a large frying pan. Add the pecans and cook, stirring, until golden. Remove from the pan and allow to cool. Coarsely chop the pecans. Add the ground cumin, garam masala, cayenne pepper and a pinch of salt to the pan, and cook for 1 minute, or until aromatic. Add the pecans and toss to coat.

Add the white rice to a pan of boiling water and simmer until tender. Drain and mix with the wild rice and pecans in a large, shallow bowl. Add the celery, tomato, spinach leaves and spring onion. Add half of the dressing and toss well. Arrange the pieces of duck on top with the skin uppermost. Drizzle with the remaining dressing and garnish with the orange zest.

note *Chinese barbecued duck can be purchased in any Chinatown, from many Asian stores or from your local Chinese restaurant.*

peanut chicken with mango

4 tablespoons eady-made satay sauce
125 ml (4 fl oz/½ cup) coconut cream
125 ml (4 fl oz/½ cup) chicken stock
2 teaspoons soy sauce
4 boneless, skinless chicken breasts,
cut into strips
plain (all-purpose) flour, for coating
2 tablespoons oil
1 large ripe mango, sliced

serves 4

method Whisk together the satay sauce, coconut cream, stock and soy sauce.

Lightly coat the chicken with flour. Heat the oil in a large deep frying pan and cook the chicken over medium heat for 4–5 minutes, or until golden brown. Remove from the pan.

Add the satay sauce mixture to the pan and bring to the boil. Boil for 3–5 minutes, or until the sauce is reduced by half. Return the chicken to the pan and heat through for 1 minute. Serve the chicken over steamed rice, topped with mango slices.

coriander and lime chicken

170 ml (6 fl oz/⅔ cup) coconut cream
125 ml (4 fl oz/½ cup) chicken stock
1½ tablespoons lime juice
2 teaspoons grated fresh ginger
4 boneless, skinless chicken breasts,
   cut into strips
plain (all-purpose) flour, for coating
2 tablespoons oil
2 tablespoons chopped coriander (cilantro)
   leaves, plus extra to garnish

serves 4

method   Whisk together the coconut cream, stock, lime juice and ginger. Lightly coat the chicken with flour.

Heat the oil in a frying pan and cook the chicken over medium heat for 4–5 minutes, or until golden brown. Remove from the pan and keep warm. Add the coconut cream mixture to the pan and bring to the boil. Cook for 5 minutes, or until reduced by half and thickened slightly.

Return the chicken to the pan, add the coriander and simmer for 1 minute to heat the chicken through. Garnish with extra coriander leaves.

chicken and cashew nuts

oil, for cooking
750 g (1 lb 10 oz) boneless, skinless chicken
thighs, cut into strips
2 egg whites, lightly beaten
60 g (2 oz/½ cup) cornflour (cornstarch)
2 onions, thinly sliced
1 red capsicum (pepper), thinly sliced
200 g (7 oz) broccoli, cut into bite-sized pieces
2 tablespoons soy sauce
2 tablespoons sherry
1 tablespoon oyster sauce
4 tablespoons roasted cashew nuts
4 spring onions (scallions), sliced diagonally

serves 4–6

method   Heat the wok until very hot, add 1 tablespoon of the oil and swirl it around to coat the side. Dip about a quarter of the chicken strips into the egg white and then into the cornflour. Add to the wok and stir-fry for 3–5 minutes, until the chicken is golden brown and just cooked. Drain on paper towels and repeat with the remaining chicken, reheating the wok and adding a little more oil each time.

Reheat the wok, add 1 tablespoon of the oil and stir-fry the onion, capsicum and broccoli over medium heat for 4–5 minutes, or until the vegetables have softened slightly. Increase the heat to high and add the soy sauce, sherry and oyster sauce. Toss the vegetables well in the sauce and bring to the boil.

Return the chicken to the wok and toss over high heat for 1–2 minutes to heat the chicken and make sure it is entirely cooked through. Season well with salt and freshly cracked black pepper. Toss the cashews and spring onion through the chicken mixture, and serve immediately.

honey chicken

oil, for cooking
500 g (1 lb 2 oz) boneless, skinless chicken
   thighs, cut into cubes
1 egg white, lightly beaten
4 tablespoons cornflour (cornstarch)
2 onions, thinly sliced
1 green capsicum (pepper), cut into squares
2 carrots, cut into batons
100 g (4 oz/1 cup) snow peas (mangetouts),
   sliced
3 tablespoons honey
2 tablespoons almonds, toasted

serves 4

method   Heat the wok until very hot, add 1½ tablespoons of the oil and swirl it around to coat the side. Dip half of the chicken into the egg white, then lightly dust with the cornflour. Stir-fry over high heat for 4–5 minutes, or until the chicken is golden brown and just cooked. Remove from the wok and drain on paper towels. Repeat with the remaining chicken, then remove all the chicken from the wok.

Reheat the wok, add 1 tablespoon of the oil and stir-fry the sliced onion over high heat for 3–4 minutes, or until slightly softened. Add the capsicum and carrot, and cook, tossing constantly, for 3–4 minutes, or until tender. Stir in the snow peas and cook for 2 minutes.

Increase the heat, add the honey and toss the vegetables until well coated. Return all of the chicken to the wok and toss until it is heated through and is well coated in the honey. Remove from the heat and season well with salt and pepper. Serve immediately, sprinkled with the almonds.

chicken with snow pea sprouts

2 tablespoons oil
1 onion, finely sliced
3 makrut (kaffir lime) leaves, shredded
3 boneless, skinless chicken breasts, diced
1 red capsicum (pepper), sliced
3 tablespoons lime juice
100 ml (4 fl oz) soy sauce
100 g (4 oz) snow pea (mangetout) sprouts
2 tablespoons chopped coriander
(cilantro) leaves

serves 4

method Heat a wok or frying pan over medium heat, add the oil and swirl to coat. Add the onion and makrut leaves and stir-fry for 3–5 minutes, or until the onion begins to soften. Add the chicken and cook for a further 4 minutes. Add the capsicum and continue to cook for 2–3 minutes.

Stir in the lime juice and soy sauce and cook for 1–2 minutes, or until the sauce reduces slightly. Add the sprouts and coriander and cook until the sprouts have wilted slightly.

variation *Use the chicken, soy sauce and lime juice as a base and add fresh asparagus, or use mint and basil instead of coriander.*

thai drumsticks

3 tablespoons Thai red curry paste
250 ml (9 fl oz/1 cup) coconut milk
2 tablespoons lime juice
4 tablespoons finely chopped coriander
    (cilantro) leaves
12 chicken drumsticks, scored
1 kg (2 lb 4 oz/2½ bunches) baby bok choy
    (pak choy)
2 tablespoons soy sauce
1 tablespoon oil

serves 6

method   Mix together the curry paste, coconut milk, lime juice and coriander. Place the chicken in a non-metallic dish and pour on the marinade. Cover and leave in the refrigerator for at least 2 hours.

Cook the chicken over medium heat on a barbecue grill plate or flat plate for 25 minutes, or until it is cooked through.

Trim the bok choy and combine with the soy sauce and oil, then cook on the barbecue or in a frying pan for 3–4 minutes, or until just wilted. Serve the chicken on a bed of bok choy.

lime steamed chicken

2 limes, thinly sliced, plus extra, to serve
4 boneless, skinless chicken breasts
500 g (1 lb 2 oz/1 bunch) bok choy (pak choy)
500 g (1 lb 2 oz/1 bunch) choy sum
1 teaspoon sesame oil
1 tablespoon peanut oil
125 ml (4 fl oz/½ cup) oyster sauce
4 tablespoons lime juice

serves 4

method Line the base of a bamboo steamer with the lime slices and place the chicken on top. Season. Place over a wok with a little water in the base, cover and steam for 8–10 minutes, or until the chicken is cooked through. Cover the chicken and keep warm. Drain and dry the wok.

Wash and trim the greens. Heat the oils in the wok and cook the greens for 2–3 minutes, or until just wilted.

Mix together the oyster sauce and lime juice and pour over the greens. Serve the chicken on top of the greens with some extra lime slices.

note *The Asian green vegetables used in this recipe, bok choy and choy sum, can be replaced by any green vegetables, such as broccoli, snow peas (mangetouts), or English spinach.*

hoisin barbecued chicken

2 garlic cloves, finely chopped
3 tablespoons hoisin sauce
3 teaspoons light soy sauce
3 teaspoons honey
1 teaspoon sesame oil
2 tablespoons tomato sauce (ketchup)
   or sweet chilli sauce
2 spring onions (scallions), finely sliced
1.5 kg (3 lb 5 oz) chicken wings

serves 4–6

method   To make the marinade, mix together the garlic, hoisin sauce, soy sauce, honey, sesame oil, tomato sauce and spring onion. Pour over the chicken wings, cover and marinate in the refrigerator for at least 2 hours.

Cook the chicken on a chargrill pan or barbecue grill plate, turning once, for 20–25 minutes, or until cooked and golden brown. Baste with the marinade during cooking. Heat any remaining marinade in a pan until boiling and serve as a sauce.

note   *The chicken can also be baked in a 180°C (350°F/Gas 4) oven for 30 minutes. Turn halfway through cooking.*

balti chicken

1 kg (2 lb 4 oz) boneless, skinless
chicken thighs
4 tablespoons oil
1 large red onion, finely chopped
4–5 garlic cloves, finely chopped
1 tablespoon grated fresh ginger
2 teaspoons ground cumin
2 teaspoons ground coriander
1 teaspoon ground turmeric
½ teaspoon chilli powder
425 g (15 oz) tin chopped tomatoes
1 green capsicum (pepper), seeded and diced
1–2 small green chillies, seeded and
finely chopped
4 tablespoons chopped coriander (cilantro)
2 spring onions (scallions), chopped, to garnish

serves 6

method Remove any excess fat or sinew from the chicken thighs and cut into four pieces.

Heat a large wok over high heat, add the oil and swirl to coat the side. Add the onion and stir-fry over medium heat for 5 minutes, or until softened but not browned. Add the garlic and ginger and stir-fry for 3 more minutes.

Add the spices, 1 teaspoon salt and 3 tablespoons water. Increase the heat to high and stir-fry for 2 minutes, or until the mixture has thickened. Take care not to burn.

Add the tomato and 250 ml (9 fl oz/1 cup) water and cook, stirring often, for a further 10 minutes, or until the mixture is thick and pulpy and the oil comes to the surface. Add the chicken to the pan, reduce the heat and simmer, stirring often, for 15 minutes. Add the capsicum and chilli and simmer for a further 25 minutes, or until the chicken is tender. Add a little water if the mixture is too thick. Stir in the coriander and garnish with the spring onion.

note *This curry is traditionally cooked in a Karahi pan—a wok is a good substitute.*

thai green chicken curry

500 ml (17 fl oz/2 cups) coconut cream
  (see Note)
4 tablespoons Thai green curry paste
2 tablespoons grated palm sugar (jaggery)
2 tablespoons fish sauce
4 makrut (kaffir lime) leaves, finely shredded
1 kg (2 lb 4 oz) boneless, skinless chicken
  thighs or breasts, cut into thick strips
200 g (7 oz) tinned bamboo shoots, cut into
  thick strips
100 g (4 oz) snake (yard-long) beans, cut
  into short lengths
1 handful Thai basil leaves, plus extra,
  to garnish

serves 4–6

method   Open the tin of coconut cream and lift off the thick cream from the top; you should have about 125 ml (4 fl oz/½ cup). Put in a wok or saucepan and bring to the boil. Add the curry paste, then reduce the heat and simmer for 15 minutes, until fragrant and the oil starts to separate from the cream. Add the palm sugar, fish sauce and makrut leaves.

Stir in the remaining coconut cream and the chicken, bamboo shoots and beans and simmer for 15 minutes, or until the chicken is tender. Stir in the Thai basil just before serving. Garnish with the extra leaves.

note   *Do not shake the tin, because good-quality coconut cream has a layer of very thick cream at the top. This has a higher fat content, which causes it to split or separate more readily than the rest of the coconut cream or milk.*

gingered duck curry

1.8 kg (4 lb) duck
1 garlic clove, crushed
1 teaspoon grated fresh ginger
1 tablespoon dark soy sauce
½ teaspoon sesame oil
8 dried Chinese mushrooms
5 cm (2 inch) piece fresh ginger, extra,
thinly sliced
2 tablespoons Thai yellow curry paste
2 tablespoons chopped lemongrass,
white part only
400 ml (14 fl oz) tin coconut milk
4 makrut (kaffir lime) leaves, shredded
100 g (4 oz) Thai pea eggplants (aubergines)
2 teaspoons soft brown sugar
2 teaspoons fish sauce
1 tablespoon lime juice

serves 4

method   Cut the duck in half by cutting down both sides of the backbone, and through the breastbone. Discard the backbone. Cut each duck half into four portions, removing any fat. Rub the duck with the combined garlic, ginger, soy sauce and oil. Refrigerate for 30 minutes.

Soak the mushrooms in boiling water for 20 minutes. Drain. Remove and discard the stalks and cut the caps in half.

Heat a lightly oiled pan. Brown the duck over medium heat. Leaving only 1 tablespoon of fat in the pan, stir-fry the extra ginger, curry paste and lemongrass for 3 minutes. Stir in the coconut milk, makrut leaves and 125 ml (4 fl oz/½ cup) water. Add the duck, cover and simmer for 45 minutes. Skim well.

Remove the eggplant stems; add the eggplants to the pan with the brown sugar, fish sauce and mushrooms. Simmer, partly covered, for 30 minutes, or until tender. Stir in juice to taste.

chicken dumplings in green curry

500 g (1 lb 2 oz) minced (ground) chicken
3 spring onions (scallions), finely chopped
2 tablespoons small coriander (cilantro) leaves
1 lemongrass stem, white part only,
  finely sliced
3 tablespoons fish sauce
1 teaspoon chicken stock (bouillon) powder
280 g (10 oz/1½ cups) cooked jasmine rice
1 egg, plus 1 egg white
2 teaspoons oil
2 tablespoons Thai green curry paste
2 x 400 ml (14 fl oz) tins coconut milk
4 fresh makrut (kaffir lime) leaves
2 very large handfuls basil leaves
1 tablespoon lemon juice

serves 4

method Mix together the chicken, spring onion, coriander leaves, lemongrass, 2 tablespoons of the fish sauce, stock powder and some pepper. Add the rice and mix well with your hands.

In a separate bowl, beat the egg and egg white with electric beaters until thick and creamy, then fold it into the chicken mixture. With lightly floured hands, roll tablespoons of the mixture into balls. Place on a tray, cover and refrigerate for 2–3 hours, or until firm.

Heat the oil in a large frying pan, add the curry paste and stir over medium heat for 1 minute. Gradually stir in the coconut milk, then reduce the heat to a simmer. Add the makrut leaves and dumplings to the sauce, cover and simmer for 25–30 minutes, stirring occasionally. Stir in the basil leaves, remaining fish sauce and lemon juice.

thai chicken and potato curry

2 tablespoons oil
1 onion, chopped
1–2 tablespoons Thai yellow curry paste
(see Notes)
¼ teaspoon ground turmeric
420 ml (15 fl oz/1⅔ cups) coconut milk
300 g (11 oz) potatoes, peeled and cubed
250 g (9 oz) orange sweet potatoes,
peeled and cubed
250 g (9 oz) boneless, skinless chicken
thighs, diced
2 makrut (kaffir lime) leaves (see Notes)
2 teaspoons fish sauce
2 teaspoons soft brown sugar
1 tablespoon lime juice
1 teaspoon lime zest
1 large handful coriander (cilantro) leaves
4 tablespoons roasted peanuts,
roughly chopped, to garnish

serves 4–6

method Heat the oil in a large heavy-based saucepan or wok and cook the onion until softened. Add the curry paste and turmeric and stir for 1 minute, or until aromatic.

Stir in the coconut milk and 250 ml (9 fl oz/1 cup) water and bring to the boil. Reduce the heat and add the potato, sweet potato, chicken and makrut leaves. Simmer for 15–20 minutes, or until the vegetables are tender and the chicken is cooked through.

Stir in the fish sauce, sugar, lime juice and zest and coriander leaves. Garnish with the peanuts to serve.

notes *Thai yellow curry paste is not as common as the red or green but is available from most Asian food stores. Makrut leaves are now available in most supermarkets.*

malaysian nonya chicken curry

curry paste

2 red onions, chopped
4 small red chillies, seeded and sliced
4 garlic cloves, sliced
2 lemongrass stems, white part only, sliced
5 cm (2 inch) piece galangal, sliced
8 makrut (kaffir lime) leaves, roughly chopped
1 teaspoon ground turmeric
½ teaspoon shrimp paste, dry-roasted

2 tablespoons oil
750 g (1 lb 10 oz) boneless, skinless chicken
    thighs, cut into bite-sized pieces
400 ml (14 fl oz) coconut milk
3 tablespoons tamarind purée
1 tablespoon fish sauce

serves 4

method   To make the curry paste, place all the ingredients in a food processor or blender and mix to a thick paste.

Heat a wok or large saucepan over high heat, add the oil and swirl to coat the side. Add the curry paste and cook, stirring occasionally, over low heat for 8–10 minutes, or until fragrant. Add the chicken and stir-fry with the paste for 2–3 minutes.

Add the coconut milk, tamarind purée and fish sauce to the wok, and simmer, stirring occasionally, for 15–20 minutes, or until the chicken is tender.

butter chicken

2 tablespoons peanut oil
1 kg (2 lb 4 oz) boneless, skinless chicken thighs, quartered
60 g (2 oz) butter or ghee
2 teaspoons garam masala
2 teaspoons sweet paprika
2 teaspoons ground coriander
1 tablespoon finely chopped fresh ginger
¼ teaspoon chilli powder
1 cinnamon stick
6 cardamom pods, bruised
350 g (12 oz) tomato passata (puréed tomatoes)
1 tablespoon sugar
3 tablespoons plain yoghurt
125 ml (4 fl oz/½ cup) cream
1 tablespoon lemon juice
coriander (cilantro) leaves, to garnish

serves 4–6

method Heat a wok until very hot, add 1 tablespoon oil and swirl to coat. Add half the chicken thighs and stir-fry for 4 minutes, or until browned. Remove. Add extra oil, as needed, and cook the remaining chicken. Remove.

Reduce the heat, add the butter or ghee to the wok and melt. Add the garam masala, sweet paprika, ground coriander, ginger, chilli powder, cinnamon stick and cardamom pods and stir-fry for 1 minute, or until fragrant. Return the chicken to the wok and mix to coat in the spices.

Add the tomato passata and sugar, and simmer, stirring, for 15 minutes, or until the chicken is tender and the sauce has thickened.

Add the yoghurt, cream and juice and simmer for 5 minutes, or until the sauce has thickened slightly. Serve with rice or poppadoms and garnish with coriander leaves.

seafood

crab and corn soup

1½ tablespoons oil

6 garlic cloves, chopped

6 red Asian shallots (eschalots), chopped

2 lemongrass stems, white part only,
   finely chopped

1 tablespoon grated fresh ginger

1 litre (35 fl oz/4 cups) chicken stock

250 ml (9 fl oz/1 cup) coconut milk

375 g (13 oz/2½ cups) frozen corn kernels

2 x 170 g (6 oz) tins crabmeat, drained

2 tablespoons fish sauce

2 tablespoons lime juice

1 teaspoon shaved palm sugar (jaggery)
   or soft brown sugar

serves 4

method   Heat the oil in a large saucepan, then add the garlic, shallots, lemongrass and ginger and cook, stirring, over medium heat for 2 minutes.

Pour the chicken stock and coconut milk into the saucepan and bring to the boil, stirring occasionally. Add the corn and cook for 5 minutes.

Add the crabmeat, fish sauce, lime juice and sugar and stir until the crab is heated through. Season to taste. Ladle into bowls and serve immediately.

crab dumpling soup

170 g (6 oz) tin crabmeat, well drained
2 tablespoons finely chopped spring
onions (scallions)
2 garlic cloves, finely chopped
2 teaspoons sesame oil
3 teaspoons chopped fresh ginger
12 small round gow gee (egg) or
won ton wrappers
3 spring onions (scallions), extra
1.25 litres (44 fl oz/5 cups) chicken stock
1 tablespoon soy sauce
1 tablespoon mirin (see Note)
1 teaspoon sugar

serves 4

method To make the crab filling, mix the crab with the chopped spring onion, half the garlic,
1 teaspoon of sesame oil and 1 teaspoon of the ginger.

Put 2 teaspoons of the filling on one half of each wrapper. Moisten the edge with some water and fold
over to form a crescent. Press the edges together firmly. Lay the dumplings on a lightly floured surface.

Cut the extra spring onions into thin strips and set aside. Heat the remaining sesame oil in a saucepan,
add the remaining garlic and ginger and cook over medium heat for 3–4 minutes, or until the garlic is
lightly golden. Add the stock, soy sauce, mirin and sugar. Bring to the boil, add the spring onion strips
(reserving some to garnish) and simmer for 2–3 minutes.

Bring a large saucepan of water to the boil, add 3–4 dumplings at a time and cook for 5 minutes, or
until just cooked. Place in bowls, ladle the stock over the dumplings, garnish with the spring onion
strips and serve.

note *Mirin is a Japanese sweetened rice wine which is used frequently in cooking.*

chilli octopus salad

1.5 kg (3 lb 5 oz) baby octopus
250 ml (9 fl oz/1 cup) sweet chilli sauce
4 tablespoons lime juice
4 tablespoons fish sauce
4 tablespoons soft brown sugar
oil, for chargrilling
200 g (7 oz) mixed salad leaves, to serve
lime wedges, to serve

serves 4

method   Cut the head from the octopus and discard. With your index finger, push the hard beak up and out of the body. Discard. Rinse the octopus under cold water, drain and pat dry.

Mix together the sweet chilli sauce, lime juice, fish sauce and sugar.

Brush a chargrill plate or barbecue grill plate with oil and heat to very hot. Cook the octopus, turning, for 3–4 minutes, or until they change colour. Brush with a quarter of the sauce during cooking. Do not overcook. Serve immediately on a bed of salad greens with the remaining sauce and the lime wedges.

japanese scallop and ginger salad

300 g (11 oz) fresh scallops, without roe
100 g (4 oz) baby English spinach leaves
1 small red capsicum (pepper),
very thinly sliced
50 g (2 oz) bean sprouts
30 ml (1 fl oz) sake
1 tablespoon lime juice
2 teaspoons shaved palm sugar (jaggery)
1 teaspoon fish sauce

serves 4

method Remove any veins, membrane or hard white muscle from the scallops. Lightly brush a chargrill pan or barbecue flat plate with oil. Cook the scallops in batches on the chargrill plate for 1 minute each side, or until just cooked.

Divide the spinach leaves, capsicum and bean sprouts among four serving plates. Arrange the scallops over the top.

To make the dressing, whisk together the sake, lime juice, palm sugar and fish sauce. Pour over the salad and serve immediately.

note *Sprinkle with toasted sesame seeds as a garnish.*

coconut prawn salad

24 raw king prawns (shrimp), peeled and
    deveined, tails left intact
plain (all-purpose) flour, to coat
1 egg
1 tablespoon milk
60 g (2 oz/1 cup) shredded coconut
2 very large handfuls chopped coriander
    (cilantro) leaves, plus 1 tablespoon extra
2½ tablespoons oil
300 g (11 oz) red Asian shallots (eschalots),
    chopped
2 garlic cloves, finely chopped
2 teaspoons grated fresh ginger
1 red chilli, seeds and membrane removed,
    thinly sliced
1 teaspoon ground turmeric
270 ml (10 fl oz) coconut cream
2 makrut (kaffir lime) leaves, thinly sliced
2 teaspoons lime juice
2 teaspoons palm sugar (jaggery)
3 teaspoons fish sauce
oil, for shallow-frying
150 g (5 oz) mixed lettuce leaves

serves 4

method   Holding the prawns by their tails, coat in flour, then dip into the combined egg and milk and then into the combined coconut and coriander. Refrigerate for 30 minutes.

Heat the oil in a saucepan and cook the shallots, garlic, ginger, chilli and turmeric over medium heat for 3–5 minutes. Add the coconut cream, makrut leaves, lime juice, palm sugar and fish sauce. Bring to the boil, then reduce the heat and simmer for 2–3 minutes, or until thick.

Heat 2 cm (3/4 inch) of the oil in a pan and cook the prawns in batches for 3–5 minutes, until golden. Drain on paper towels and season. Add the coriander to the dressing. Toss the lettuce and prawns together and drizzle with the dressing.

soba noodles with salmon and miso

300 g (11 oz) soba noodles
1 tablespoon soya bean oil
3 teaspoons white miso paste
100 g (4 oz) honey
1½ tablespoons sesame oil
6 salmon fillets, skin and bones removed
1 teaspoon chopped garlic
1 tablespoon grated fresh ginger
1 carrot, cut into matchsticks
6 small spring onions (scallions), thinly sliced
60 g (2 oz/1 cup) soya bean sprouts
4 tablespoons rice vinegar
3 tablespoons light soy sauce
1 teaspoon sesame oil, extra
1 tablespoon sesame seeds, toasted
mustard cress, to serve

serves 6

method Preheat the oven to moderate 180°C (350°F/Gas 4). Fill a large saucepan three-quarters full with water and bring to the boil. Add the noodles and return to the boil. Cook for 1 minute, then add 250 ml (9 fl oz/1 cup) cold water. Boil for 1–2 minutes, then add another 250 ml (9 fl oz/1 cup) water. Boil for 2 minutes, or until tender, then drain and toss with ½ teaspoon of the soya bean oil.

Whisk together the miso, honey, sesame oil and 1 tablespoon water to form a paste. Brush over the salmon, then sear on a hot chargrill or frying pan for 30 seconds on each side. Brush the salmon with the remaining paste and place on a baking tray. Bake for 6 minutes, then cover and leave to rest in a warm place.

Heat the remaining soya bean oil in a wok. Add the garlic, ginger, carrot, spring onion and sprouts and stir-fry for 1 minute—the vegetables should not brown, but remain crisp. Add the noodles, rice vinegar, soy sauce and extra sesame oil and stir-fry quickly to heat through.

Divide the noodles among six serving plates, top with a portion of salmon and sprinkle with sesame seeds. Garnish with the mustard cress before serving.

tuna in makrut sauce

375 ml (13 fl oz/1½ cups) cream
375 ml (13 fl oz/1½ cups) fish stock
12 makrut (kaffir lime) leaves, finely sliced
2 tablespoons peanut oil
4 small tuna steaks, cubed
1 kg (2 lb 4 oz/2½ bunches) baby bok choy
   (pak choy), halved
lime wedges, to serve

serves 4

method   Place the cream, fish stock and makrut leaves in a small saucepan over low heat. Boil for 15 minutes, stirring occasionally, or until the sauce has reduced and thickened. Keep warm.

Meanwhile, heat a wok until very hot, add the oil and swirl to coat the side. Add the tuna, in batches if necessary, and stir-fry for 2 minutes, or until seared on all sides but not cooked through. Remove the tuna. Add the bok choy to the wok and stir-fry over high heat for 1–2 minutes, or until the leaves begin to wilt. Add 1–2 teaspoons water, if necessary, to assist wilting.

Place the bok choy and tuna on a serving plate and pour on the sauce. Serve with lime wedges.

sesame-coated tuna with coriander salsa

4 tuna steaks
120 g (4 oz/¾ cup) sesame seeds
100 g (4 oz) baby rocket (arugula) leaves

coriander salsa

2 tomatoes, seeded and diced
1 large garlic clove, crushed
2 tablespoons finely chopped coriander
(cilantro) leaves
2 tablespoons virgin olive oil, plus extra
for shallow-frying
1 tablespoon lime juice

serves 4

method Cut each tuna steak into three pieces. Put the sesame seeds on a sheet of baking paper. Roll the tuna in the sesame seeds to coat. Refrigerate for 15 minutes.

To make the salsa, mix together the tomato, garlic, coriander, olive oil and lime juice. Cover and refrigerate until ready to serve.

Fill a heavy-based frying pan to 1.5 cm (⅝ inch) deep with the extra oil and place over high heat. Add the tuna in two batches and cook for 2 minutes each side. Remove and drain on paper towels. Divide the rocket among four plates, top with the tuna and serve with the salsa.

chilli crab

1 kg (2 lb 4 oz) raw blue swimmer crabs
2 tablespoons peanut oil
2 garlic cloves, finely chopped
2 teaspoons finely chopped fresh ginger
2 small red chillies, seeded and sliced
   (see Note)
2 tablespoons hoisin sauce
125 ml (4 fl oz/½ cup) tomato sauce (ketchup)
3 tablespoons sweet chilli sauce
1 tablespoon fish sauce
½ teaspoon sesame oil
4 spring onions (scallions), finely sliced,
   to garnish, optional

serves 4

method   Pull back the apron and remove the top shell from each crab. Remove the intestines and grey feathery gills. Segment each crab into four pieces. Crack the claws open with a crab cracker to allow the flavours to enter the crabmeat and also to make it easier to eat the crab.

Heat a wok until very hot, add the oil and swirl to coat. Add the garlic, ginger and chilli and stir-fry for 1–2 minutes.

Add the crab pieces and stir-fry for 5–7 minutes, or until the meat turns white. Stir in the hoisin, tomato, sweet chilli and fish sauces, the sesame oil and 3 tablespoons of water. Bring to the boil, then reduce the heat and simmer, covered, for 6 minutes, or until the crab flesh is cooked through and flakes easily. Garnish with spring onion and serve with finger bowls.

notes   *If you prefer a hotter sauce, leave the seeds and membrane in the chillies. You can use any variety of raw crabmeat for this recipe, or use prawns (shrimp) instead.*

salmon with asian greens and chilli jam

chilli jam

2½ tablespoons vegetable oil
1 large onion, thinly sliced
6 red bird's eye chillies, seeded and thinly sliced
2 teaspoons grated fresh ginger
185 ml (6 fl oz/¾ cup) white wine vinegar
150 g (5 oz/¾ cup) soft brown sugar
2 teaspoons lime juice

1 tablespoon peanut oil
1 red capsicum (pepper), thinly sliced
500 g (1 lb 2 oz/1½ bunches) baby bok choy (pak choy), quartered
1 garlic clove, finely chopped
1 tablespoon soy sauce
1 teaspoon sugar
1 tablespoon oil
4 salmon cutlets

serves 4

method To make the chilli jam, heat the oil in a saucepan and add the onion, chilli and ginger. Cook over medium heat for 3–4 minutes, or until the onion is soft. Add the remaining ingredients and 3 tablespoons water and stir until the sugar dissolves. Bring to the boil, then reduce the heat. Simmer for 35–40 minutes, until thick and pulpy. Cool slightly and mix until smooth in a food processor. Cool.

Heat the peanut oil in a frying pan, add the capsicum and cook over medium heat for 2 minutes, then add the bok choy and cook for 1 minute. Add the garlic and cook until fragrant. Reduce the heat, add the soy sauce and sugar and warm. Remove from the heat. Keep warm.

Heat the oil in a frying pan, season the salmon and cook over medium heat for 2 minutes each side, or until cooked to your liking. Serve with the vegetables and jam.

teriyaki tuna with wasabi mayonnaise

125 ml (4 fl oz/½ cup) teriyaki marinade
½ teaspoon five-spice
1 tablespoon grated fresh ginger
3 tuna steaks, each cut into 4 strips
2 tablespoons peanut oil
3 tablespoons mayonnaise
1 teaspoon wasabi paste
2 tablespoons pickled ginger, to serve

serves 4

method Combine the teriyaki marinade, five-spice powder and ginger. Place the tuna in a non-metallic dish, pour over the marinade, cover and leave to marinate for 10 minutes. Drain and discard the marinade.

Heat the oil in a large non-stick frying pan. Add the tuna, in batches if necessary, and cook over high heat for 1–2 minutes each side, or until cooked to your liking. The time will vary depending on the thickness of the fish.

Mix together the mayonnaise and wasabi paste. Serve the tuna steaks with wasabi mayonnaise and a little pickled ginger.

2 t

2 s

serves 4

method Open out the squid tubes. Lightly score a diamond pattern over the inside surface of each, then cut into 5 cm (2 inch) squares.

For the sauce, mix the cornflour with 125 ml (4 fl oz/½ cup) water. Mash the black beans with a fork. Add the chilli, garlic, ginger, oyster and soy sauces, sugar and the cornflour mixture and stir well.

Heat the oil in a wok or frying pan and stir-fry the onion for 1 minute over high heat. Add the capsicum and corn and cook for another 2 minutes.

Add the squid to the wok and stir for 1–2 minutes, until it curls up. Add the sauce and bring to the boil, stirring until the sauce thickens. Stir in the spring onion.

note *Black beans are available in cans in Asian food stores.*

lemongrass and coriander fish

4 x 200 g (7 oz) fish cutlets
plain (all-purpose) flour, seasoned with salt
    and pepper
2–3 tablespoons peanut oil
2 onions, sliced
2 lemongrass stems, white part only,
    finely chopped
4 makrut (kaffir lime) leaves, finely shredded
1 teaspoon ground cumin
1 teaspoon ground coriander
1 teaspoon finely chopped red chilli
185 ml (6 fl oz/¾ cup) chicken stock
375 ml (13 fl oz/1½ cups) coconut milk
1 very large handful fresh coriander (cilantro),
    chopped
2 teaspoons fish sauce

serves 4

method Preheat the oven to 180°C (350°F/Gas 4). Toss the fish lightly in the flour. Heat half the oil in a large heavy-based frying pan and cook the fish over medium heat until lightly browned on both sides. Transfer to a shallow ovenproof dish.

Heat the remaining oil in the pan. Cook the onion and lemongrass, stirring, for 5 minutes, or until the onion softens. Add the makrut leaves, ground spices and chilli and stir for about 2 minutes, or until fragrant.

Add the stock and coconut milk and bring to the boil. Pour over the fish, then cover and bake for 30 minutes, or until tender. Transfer to a plate.

Stir the coriander and fish sauce into the remaining sauce and season to taste. Pour over the fish to serve.

note *Makrut leaves are glossy, dark green double leaves with a floral citrus smell. They are tough and need to be finely shredded before use.*

100 EASY RECIPES ASIAN

japanese-style salmon parcels

2 teaspoons sesame seeds
4 x 150 g (5 oz) salmon cutlets or steaks
2.5 cm (1 inch) piece fresh ginger
2 celery stalks
4 spring onions (scallions)
3 tablespoons mirin (see Note)
2 tablespoons tamari
¼ teaspoon dashi granules

serves 4

method Cut baking paper into four squares large enough to wrap the salmon steaks. Preheat the oven to 230°C (450°F/Gas 8). Lightly toast the sesame seeds under a grill (broiler) or in the oven for a few minutes.

Wash the salmon and dry with paper towels. Place a salmon cutlet in the centre of each paper square.

Cut the ginger into paper-thin slices. Slice the celery stalks and spring onions into short lengths, then lengthways into fine strips. Arrange a bundle of the prepared strips and several slices of ginger on each salmon steak.

Combine the mirin, tamari and dashi granules in a small saucepan. Heat gently until the dashi granules dissolve. Drizzle over each parcel, sprinkle with sesame seeds and carefully wrap the salmon, folding in the sides to seal in all the juices. Arrange the parcels on a baking tray and cook for about 12 minutes, or until tender. (The paper will puff up when the fish is cooked.) Do not overcook or the salmon will dry out. Serve immediately, as standing time can spoil the fish.

note *Mirin, tamari and dashi are all available from Japanese food stores.*

malaysian fish curry

5 cm (2 inch) piece fresh ginger
3–6 medium red chillies
1 onion, chopped
4 garlic cloves, chopped
3 lemongrass stems, white part only, sliced
2 teaspoons shrimp paste
3 tablespoons oil
1 tablespoon fish curry powder (see Note)
250 ml (9 fl oz/1 cup) coconut milk
1 tablespoon tamarind concentrate
1 tablespoon kecap manis (see Note, page 28)
500 g (1 lb 2 oz) firm white skinless fish fillets,
  cut into cubes
2 ripe tomatoes, chopped
1 tablespoon lemon juice

serves 4

method   Slice the ginger and mix in a small food processor with the chillies, onion, garlic, lemongrass and shrimp paste until roughly chopped. Add 2 tablespoons of the oil and process until paste forms, regularly scraping the side of the bowl with a spatula.

Heat the remaining oil in a wok or deep, heavy-based frying pan and add the paste. Cook for 3–4 minutes over low heat, stirring constantly, until the paste is fragrant. Add the curry powder and stir for 2 minutes. Add the coconut milk, tamarind, kecap manis and 250 ml (9 fl oz/1 cup) water. Bring to the boil, stirring occasionally, then reduce the heat and simmer for 10 minutes.

Add the fish, tomato and lemon juice. Season to taste, then simmer for 5 minutes, until the fish is just cooked (it will flake easily).

note   *Fish curry powder blend is available from speciality stores.*

thai prawn curry

5 cm (2 inch) piece galangal
1 small onion, roughly chopped
3 garlic cloves
4 dried long red chillies
4 whole black peppercorns
2 tablespoons chopped lemongrass, white part only
1 tablespoon chopped coriander (cilantro) root
2 teaspoons grated lime zest
2 teaspoons cumin seeds
1 teaspoon sweet paprika
1 teaspoon ground coriander
3 tablespoons oil
1–2 tablespoons fish sauce
2 makrut (kaffir lime) leaves
500 ml (17 fl oz/2 cups) coconut cream
1 kg (2 lb 4 oz) raw prawns (shrimp), peeled and deveined

serves 4

method Peel the galangal and thinly slice. Mix the onion, garlic, chillies, peppercorns, lemongrass, coriander root, lime zest, cumin seeds, paprika, ground coriander, 2 tablespoons oil and 1/2 teaspoon salt in a food processor until a smooth paste forms.

Heat the remaining oil in a frying pan. Add half the curry paste and stir over medium heat for 2 minutes. Stir in the fish sauce, galangal, makrut leaves and coconut cream.

Add the prawns to the pan and simmer for 5 minutes, or until the prawns are cooked and the sauce has thickened slightly.

note *Left-over curry paste can be kept in the refrigerator for up to 2 weeks. It can also be frozen for up to 2 months.*

thai green fish curry

1 tablespoon peanut oil
1 onion, chopped
1½ tablespoons Thai green curry paste
375 ml (13 fl oz/1½ cups) coconut milk
750 g (1 lb 10 oz) boneless firm white
    fish fillets, cut into bite-sized pieces
3 makrut (kaffir lime) leaves
1 tablespoon fish sauce
2 teaspoons grated palm sugar (jaggery)
2 tablespoons lime juice
1 long green chilli, finely sliced

serves 4

method Heat a wok until very hot, add the oil and swirl to coat. Add the onion and stir-fry for 2 minutes, or until soft. Add the curry paste and stir-fry for 1–2 minutes, or until fragrant. Stir in the coconut milk and bring to the boil.

Add the fish and makrut leaves to the wok, reduce the heat and simmer, stirring occasionally, for 8–10 minutes, or until the fish is cooked through.

Stir in the fish sauce, palm sugar and lime juice. Scatter the chilli slices over the curry before serving.

prawn and coconut curry

1 onion, chopped
2 garlic cloves, crushed
1 lemongrass stem, white part only,
finely chopped
½ teaspoon sambal oelek (South-East
Asian chilli paste)
2 teaspoons garam masala
4 makrut (kaffir lime) leaves, finely shredded
3 tablespoons chopped coriander
(cilantro) stems
1 tablespoon peanut oil
250 ml (9 fl oz/1 cup) chicken stock
400 ml (14 fl oz) coconut milk
1 kg (2 lb 4 oz) raw prawns (shrimp), peeled
and deveined
1 tablespoon fish sauce

serves 4

method To make the curry paste, mix the onion, garlic, lemongrass, sambal oelek, garam masala, makrut leaves, coriander stems and 2 tablespoons water in a food processor until smooth.

Heat the oil in a saucepan, add the curry paste and cook for 2–3 minutes, or until fragrant. Stir in the stock and coconut milk, bring to the boil, then reduce the heat and simmer for 10 minutes, or until slightly thickened.

Add the prawns and cook for 3–5 minutes, or until cooked through. Stir in the fish sauce.

variation *Instead of prawns, you can use bite-sized pieces of boneless ling or gemfish fillets. Cook for 3–5 minutes, or until cooked through.*

vegetables

spicy indian lentil salad

210 g (8 oz/heaped 1 cup) brown rice
185 g (7 oz/1 cup) brown lentils
1 teaspoon turmeric
1 teaspoon ground cinnamon
6 cardamom pods
3 star anise
2 bay leaves
3 tablespoons sunflower oil
1 tablespoon lemon juice
250 g (9 oz) broccoli florets
2 carrots, cut into matchsticks
1 onion, finely chopped
2 garlic cloves, crushed
1 red capsicum (pepper), finely chopped
1 teaspoon garam masala
1 teaspoon ground coriander
235 g (9 oz/1½ cups) peas

mint and yoghurt dressing

250 g (9 oz/1 cup) plain yoghurt
1 tablespoon lemon juice
1 tablespoon finely chopped mint
1 teaspoon cumin seeds

serves 6

method   Put 750 ml (26 fl oz/3 cups) water with the rice, lentils, turmeric, cinnamon, cardamom, star anise and bay leaves in a saucepan. Stir to mix and bring to the boil. Reduce the heat, then cover and simmer for 50–60 minutes. Remove the whole spices and discard. Transfer the mixture to a bowl. Whisk 2 tablespoons of the oil with the lemon juice and fork through the rice mixture.

Cook the broccoli and carrot until tender. Heat the remaining oil in a large saucepan and stir-fry the onion, garlic and capsicum for 2–3 minutes, then add the garam masala and ground coriander. Cook for 1–2 minutes. Add the vegetables and toss to coat. Add to the rice mixture and fork through to combine. Cover and refrigerate.

To make the dressing, mix all the ingredients, and season with salt and pepper. Serve the salad with the dressing.

100 EASY RECIPES ASIAN

japanese spinach salad

2 eggs
1 sheet nori (dried seaweed),
cut into matchsticks
100 g (4 oz) baby English spinach leaves
1 small red onion, finely sliced
½ small daikon radish, finely sliced
2 Lebanese (short) cucumbers, sliced
30 g (1 oz) pickled ginger, sliced
1 tablespoon toasted sesame seeds

dressing

4 tablespoons light olive oil
1 tablespoon rice vinegar
1 tablespoon light soy sauce

serves 4

method Preheat the grill (broiler) to hot. Beat the eggs lightly in a small bowl, add 1 tablespoon water and the nori. Season well. Heat and grease a 20 cm (8 inch) omelette pan. Pour in the mixture to make a thin omelette. When lightly browned underneath, place under the grill (broiler) to set the top, without colouring. Turn out onto a board and leave to cool. Cut the omelette into thin strips.

To make the dressing, whisk together the olive oil, vinegar and soy sauce until combined.

Toss the spinach leaves, onion, daikon, cucumber, ginger, sesame seeds, omelette strips and dressing together in a large bowl.

basmati rice, cashew and pea salad

40 g (1½ oz) butter or ghee
½ teaspoon turmeric
300 g (11 oz/1½ cups) basmati rice
200 g (7 oz/1¼ cups) peas
3 tablespoons peanut oil
1 teaspoon yellow mustard seeds
1 teaspoon cumin seeds
3 tablespoons currants
1 garlic clove, crushed
1–2 small green chillies, finely chopped
1 teaspoon madras curry powder
100 ml (4 fl oz) coconut cream
50 g (2 oz) glacé (candied) ginger, cut
    into thin strips
¼ small red onion, finely chopped
1 tablespoon chopped mint leaves
1 tablespoon chopped coriander (cilantro)
30 g (1 oz/½ cup) shredded coconut
100 g (4 oz/⅔ cup) roasted cashew nuts,
    coarsely chopped
2 teaspoons shredded coconut, to garnish

serves 6

method   Melt the butter in a heavy-based saucepan and stir in the turmeric. Add the rice and ½ teaspoon salt, and stir for 10–15 seconds, then pour in 375 ml (13 fl oz/1½ cups) water. Stir over high heat until boiling, then reduce the heat until gently simmering. Simmer, covered, for 13 minutes without removing the lid. Remove the pan from the heat and set aside, covered, for 10 minutes, then fluff gently with a fork. Add the peas, transfer to a large bowl and allow to cool.

Heat 2 teaspoons of the oil in a saucepan and stir in the mustard and cumin seeds. When the mustard seeds start to pop, add the currants, garlic, chilli and curry powder. Stir to combine, but do not brown. Stir in the coconut cream, remove from the heat and transfer to the bowl of rice and peas.

Add the ginger, onion, herbs and the remaining oil to the rice and peas. Toss well, and set aside for at least 30 minutes. Just before serving, toss through the coconut and cashew nuts. Garnish with the shredded coconut.

note   *Rice salads often improve if made in advance. This dish may be prepared up to 24 hours in advance, but add the cashew nuts and shredded coconut just before serving to keep them crisp.*

gado gado

6 new potatoes
2 carrots, cut into thick batons
250 g (9 oz) snake beans, cut into long lengths
2 tablespoons peanut oil
250 g (9 oz) firm tofu, cubed
100 g (4 oz) baby English spinach leaves
2 Lebanese (short) cucumbers, cut into batons
1 large red capsicum (pepper), cut into batons
100 g (4 oz) bean sprouts
5 hard-boiled eggs

peanut sauce

1 tablespoon peanut oil
1 onion, finely chopped
150 g (5 oz/$\frac{2}{3}$ cup) peanut butter
3 tablespoons kecap manis
(see Note, page 28)
2 tablespoons ground coriander
2 teaspoons chilli sauce
185 ml (6 fl oz/$\frac{3}{4}$ cup) coconut cream
1 teaspoon grated palm sugar (jaggery)
1 tablespoon lemon juice

serves 4

method   Boil the potatoes until tender. Drain and cool slightly. Cut into quarters. Cook the carrot and beans separately in boiling water until just tender. Plunge into iced water, then drain.

Heat the oil in a non-stick frying pan and cook the tofu in batches. Drain on paper towels.

To make the peanut sauce, heat the oil in a frying pan over low heat and cook the onion for about 5 minutes. Add the peanut butter, kecap manis, coriander, chilli sauce and coconut cream. Bring to the boil, reduce the heat and simmer for 5 minutes. Stir in the palm sugar and juice until the sugar has dissolved.

Arrange the vegetables and tofu on a plate. Halve the eggs and place in the centre. Serve with the peanut sauce.

bok choy salad

250 ml (9 fl oz/1 cup) chicken stock
1 small carrot, cut into matchsticks
4 baby bok choy (pak choy)
100 g (4 oz/1 cup) snow peas (mangetouts),
   thinly sliced
90 g (3 oz/1 cup) bean sprouts, trimmed
1 tablespoon chopped coriander (cilantro)

sesame dressing

4 tablespoons peanut oil
1 teaspoon sesame oil
1 tablespoon white vinegar
1 tablespoon sesame seeds, toasted (see Hint)
2 teaspoons grated fresh ginger
2 teaspoons honey, warmed
1 garlic clove, crushed

serves 4

method   Pour the chicken stock into a frying pan and bring to the boil. Add the carrot and the bok choy, cover and cook for 2 minutes. Drain the vegetables and leave to cool, then halve the bok choy lengthways.

To make the dressing, whisk together the oils, vinegar, sesame seeds, ginger, honey and garlic. Season with salt and pepper, to taste.

Place the cooled carrot strips and halved bok choy in a large serving dish and arrange the snow peas, bean sprouts and coriander on top. Drizzle with the sesame dressing.

hint *To toast the sesame seeds, place in a dry pan and shake gently over medium heat until the seeds smell fragrant and begin to turn a pale golden colour. Turn the seeds out onto a plate and leave to cool.*

tempeh stir-fry

1 teaspoon sesame oil
1 tablespoon peanut oil
2 garlic cloves, crushed
1 tablespoon grated fresh ginger
1 red chilli, finely sliced
4 spring onions (scallions), sliced on
the diagonal
300 g (11 oz) tempeh, diced
500 g (1 lb 2 oz) baby bok choy
(pak choy) leaves
800 g (1 lb 12 oz) Chinese broccoli, chopped
125 ml (4 fl oz/½ cup) mushroom oyster sauce
2 tablespoons rice vinegar
2 tablespoons coriander (cilantro) leaves
3 tablespoons toasted cashew nuts

serves 4

method Heat the oils in a wok over high heat, add the garlic, ginger, chilli and spring onion and cook for 1–2 minutes, or until the onion is soft. Add the tempeh and cook for 5 minutes, or until golden. Remove and keep warm.

Add half the greens and 1 tablespoon water to the wok and cook, covered, for 3–4 minutes, or until wilted. Remove and repeat with the remaining greens and more water.

Return the greens and tempeh to the wok, add the sauce and vinegar and warm through. Top with the coriander and cashew nuts. Serve with rice.

asian greens with teriyaki tofu dressing

650 g (1 lb 7 oz) baby bok choy (pak choy)
500 g (1 lb 2 oz) choy sum
440 g (15 oz) snake (yard-long) beans,
    topped and tailed
3 tablespoons oil
1 onion, thinly sliced
4 tablespoons soft brown sugar
½ teaspoon ground chilli
2 tablespoons grated fresh ginger
250 ml (9 fl oz/1 cup) teriyaki sauce
1 tablespoon sesame oil
600 g (1 lb 5 oz) silken firm tofu, drained

serves 6

method Cut the the baby bok choy and choy sum widthways into thirds. Cut the beans into 10 cm (4 inch) lengths.

Heat a wok over high heat, add 1 tablespoon of the oil and swirl to coat the side. Cook the onion in batches for 3–5 minutes, or until crisp. Remove with a slotted spoon and drain on paper towels.

Heat 1 tablespoon of the oil in the wok, add half the greens and stir-fry for 2–3 minutes, or until wilted. Remove and keep warm. Repeat with the remaining oil and greens, then remove and drain any liquid from the wok.

Add the combined sugar, chilli, ginger and teriyaki sauce to the wok and bring to the boil. Simmer for 1 minute. Add the sesame oil and tofu and simmer for 2 minutes, turning once—the tofu will break up. Divide the greens among serving plates, then top with the dressing. Sprinkle with the fried onion.

sweet and sour tofu

600 g (1 lb 5 oz) firm tofu
3–4 tablespoons soya bean oil
1 large carrot, cut into matchsticks
150 g (5 oz/1⅔ cups) trimmed bean sprouts or
soya bean sprouts
90 g (3 oz/1 cup) sliced button mushrooms
6–8 spring onions (scallions), cut diagonally
100 g (4 oz) snow peas (mangetouts),
cut in half diagonally
4 tablespoons rice vinegar
2 tablespoons light soy sauce
1½ tablespoons caster (superfine) sugar
2 tablespoons tomato sauce (ketchup)
375 ml (13 fl oz/1½ cups) chicken or
vegetable stock
1 tablespoon cornflour (cornstarch)

serves 4

method Cut the tofu in half horizontally, then cut into 16 triangles in total. Heat 2 tablespoons of the oil in a frying pan. Add the tofu in batches and cook over medium heat for 2 minutes on each side, or until crisp and golden. Drain on paper towels. Keep warm.

Wipe the pan clean and heat the remaining oil. Add the carrot, bean sprouts, mushrooms, spring onion and snow peas and stir-fry for 1 minute. Add the vinegar, soy sauce, sugar, tomato sauce and stock and cook for a further 1 minute.

Combine the cornflour with 2 tablespoons water. Add to the vegetable mixture and cook until the sauce thickens. Serve the tofu with the sauce poured over the top.

tofu in black bean sauce

4 tablespoons vegetable stock
2 teaspoons cornflour (cornstarch)
2 teaspoons Chinese rice wine (see Note)
1 teaspoon sesame oil
1 tablespoon soy sauce
2 tablespoons peanut oil
450 g (1 lb) firm tofu, cubed
2 garlic cloves, very finely chopped
2 teaspoons finely chopped fresh ginger
3 tablespoons fermented black beans, rinsed
   and very finely chopped
4 spring onions (scallions), cut on the diagonal
1 red capsicum (pepper), cut into squares
300 g (11 oz) baby bok choy (pak choy),
   chopped

serves 4

method   Combine the vegetable stock, cornflour, rice wine, sesame oil, soy sauce, 1/2 teaspoon salt and freshly ground black pepper in a small bowl.

Heat a wok over medium heat, add the peanut oil and swirl to coat. Add the tofu and stir-fry in two batches for 3 minutes each batch, or until lightly browned. Remove with a slotted spoon and drain on paper towels. Discard any bits of tofu stuck to the wok or floating in the oil.

Add the garlic and ginger and stir-fry for 30 seconds. Toss in the black beans and spring onion and stir-fry for 30 seconds. Add the capsicum and stir-fry for 1 minute. Add the bok choy and stir-fry for a further 2 minutes.

Return the tofu to the wok and stir gently. Pour in the sauce and stir gently for 2–3 minutes, or until the sauce has thickened slightly. Serve immediately.

note   *Chinese rice wine is an alcoholic liquid made from cooked glutinous rice and millet mash which has been fermented with yeast, then aged for a period of 10 to 100 years. With a sherry-like taste, it is used as both a drink and a cooking liquid.*

cauliflower curry

marinade

1 large onion, roughly chopped
1 teaspoon grated fresh ginger
2 garlic cloves, crushed
3 green chillies, chopped
3 tablespoons plain yoghurt

1 cauliflower, divided into florets
oil, for deep-frying

curry sauce

2 tablespoons ghee
1 onion, finely chopped
2 tablespoons tomato paste
(concentrated purée)
2 tablespoons cream
1 teaspoon chilli powder
1½ tablespoons garam masala

serves 6

method To make the marinade, place all the ingredients in a food processor and mix until smooth. Place the marinade in a bowl, add the cauliflower, toss to coat and leave for 30 minutes.

Fill a deep heavy-based saucepan one-third full of oil and heat to 160°C (315°F), or until a cube of bread dropped into the oil browns in 30–35 seconds. Cook the cauliflower in batches for 30 seconds until golden brown all over. Drain on paper towels.

To make the curry sauce, heat the ghee in a frying pan, add the onion and cook for 4–5 minutes, or until soft. Add the tomato paste, cream, chilli powder, garam masala, 375 ml (13 fl oz/1½ cups) water and salt to taste. Cook, stirring constantly, over medium heat for 3 minutes.

Add the cauliflower to the sauce and cook for 7 minutes, adding some water if the sauce becomes dry.

thai red vegetable curry

1 tablespoon peanut oil
250 g (9 oz) broccoli florets, quartered
250 g (9 oz) cauliflower florets, quartered
500 g (1 lb 2 oz) orange sweet potato, cut into
    even-size chunks
2 tablespoons Thai red curry paste
500 ml (17 fl oz/2 cups) coconut milk
1 tablespoon lime juice
1 tablespoon fish sauce, optional
3 tablespoons chopped coriander (cilantro)

serves 4

method Heat a wok over high heat, add the oil and swirl to coat the side. Add the broccoli, cauliflower and sweet potato in batches and stir-fry for 3 minutes. Add 3 tablespoons water and cover. Reduce the heat to low for 8–10 minutes to steam the vegetables.

Add the red curry paste and cook over medium heat for 30 seconds, or until fragrant. Stir in the coconut milk and simmer for 8 minutes, or until slightly thickened. Add the lime juice, fish sauce and coriander.

chickpea curry

220 g (8 oz/1 cup) dried chickpeas
2 tablespoons oil
2 onions, finely chopped
2 large ripe tomatoes, chopped
½ teaspoon ground coriander
1 teaspoon ground cumin
1 teaspoon chilli powder
¼ teaspoon ground turmeric
1 tablespoon channa (chole) masala
(see Note)
1 tablespoon ghee or butter
1 small white onion, sliced, to garnish
mint and coriander (cilantro) leaves, to garnish

serves 6

method Place the chickpeas in a bowl, cover with water and leave to soak overnight. Drain, rinse and place in a large saucepan. Cover with plenty of water and bring to the boil, then reduce the heat and simmer for 40 minutes, or until tender. Drain.

Heat the oil in a large saucepan, add the onion and cook over medium heat for 15 minutes, or until golden brown. Add the tomato, ground coriander and cumin, chilli powder, turmeric and channa masala. Add 500 ml (17 fl oz/2 cups) water and cook for 10 minutes, or until the tomato is soft. Add the chickpeas, season well with salt and cook for 7–10 minutes, or until the sauce thickens. Transfer to a serving dish. Place the ghee or butter on top and allow to melt before serving. Garnish with the sliced onion and fresh mint and coriander leaves.

note *Channa (chole) masala is a spice blend specifically used in this dish. It is available at Indian grocery stores. Garam masala can be used as a substitute, but this will alter the final flavour.*

green curry with sweet potato and eggplant

1 tablespoon oil
1 onion, chopped
1–2 tablespoons Thai green curry paste
1 eggplant (aubergine), quartered and sliced
375 ml (13 fl oz/1½ cups) coconut milk
250 ml (9 fl oz/1 cup) vegetable stock
6 makrut (kaffir lime) leaves
1 orange sweet potato, cut into cubes
2 teaspoons soft brown sugar
2 tablespoons lime juice
2 teaspoons lime zest

serves 4–6

method Heat the oil in a large wok or frying pan. Add the onion and curry paste and cook, stirring, over medium heat for 3 minutes. Add the eggplant and cook for a further 4–5 minutes, or until softened.

Pour in the coconut milk and vegetable stock, bring to the boil, then reduce the heat and simmer for 5 minutes. Add the makrut leaves and sweet potato and cook, stirring occasionally, for 10 minutes, or until the eggplant and sweet potato are very tender.

Mix in the brown sugar, lime juice and lime zest until well combined with the vegetables. Season to taste with salt.

tofu with cucumber and wakame salad

3 Lebanese (short) cucumbers, thinly sliced
20 g (1 oz) dried wakame
500 g (1 lb 2 oz) silken firm tofu
3 tablespoons shiro miso
1 tablespoon mirin
1 tablespoon sugar
1 tablespoon rice vinegar
1 egg yolk
100 g (4 oz) bean sprouts, blanched
2 tablespoons sesame seeds, toasted

dressing

3 tablespoons rice vinegar
¼ teaspoon soy sauce
1½ tablespoons sugar
1 tablespoon mirin

serves 4

method Sprinkle the cucumber generously with salt and leave for 20 minutes, or until very soft, then rinse and drain. To rehydrate the wakame, soak in cold water for 20–30 minutes, then drain well.

Place the tofu in a colander, weigh down with a plate and leave to drain.

Place the shiro miso, mirin, sugar, rice vinegar and 2 tablespoons water in a saucepan and stir over low heat for 1 minute, or until the sugar dissolves. Remove from the heat, then add the egg yolk and whisk until glossy. Cool slightly.

Cut the tofu into thick sticks and place on a non-stick baking tray. Brush the miso mixture over the tofu and cook under a hot grill (broiler) for 6 minutes each side, or until light golden on both sides.

To make the dressing, place all the ingredients and ½ teaspoon salt in a bowl and whisk together well.

To assemble, place the cucumber in the centre of a plate, top with the sprouts and wakame, drizzle with the dressing, top with the tofu and serve sprinkled with the sesame seeds.

note *Wakame is an edible seaweed. Shiro miso (white miso) is fermented paste of soy beans and usually either barley or rice. Both are available from Asian grocery stores and some supermarkets.*

Published in 2010 by Bay Books,
an imprint of Murdoch Books Pty Limited

Murdoch Books Australia
Pier 8/9
23 Hickson Road
Millers Point NSW 2000
Phone: +61 (0) 2 8220 2000
Fax: +61 (0) 2 8220 2558
www.murdochbooks.com.au

Murdoch Books UK Limited
Erico House, 6th Floor
93–99 Upper Richmond Road
Putney, London SW15 2TG
Phone: +44 (0) 20 8785 5995
Fax: +44 (0) 20 8785 5985
www.murdochbooks.co.uk

Chief Executive: Juliet Rogers

Publisher: Lynn Lewis
Senior Designer: Heather Menzies
Designer: Pinch Me Design
Editor: Zoë Harpham
Editorial Coordinator: Liz Malcolm
Index: Jo Rudd
Production: Alexandra Gonzalez

ISBN: 978-1-74266-165-0

Printed by C & C Offset Printing Co. Ltd, China.

IMPORTANT: Those who might be at risk from the effects of salmonella poisoning (the elderly, pregnant women, young children and those suffering from immune deficiency diseases) should consult their doctor with any concerns about eating raw eggs.

OVEN GUIDE: You may find cooking times vary depending on the oven you are using. For fan-forced ovens, as a general rule, set the oven temperature to 20°C (35°F) lower than indicated in the recipe.